Reconciling and Rehumanizing Indigenous–Settler Relations

Reconciling and Rehumanizing Indigenous–Settler Relations

An Applied Anthropological Perspective

Nadia Ferrara

LEXINGTON BOOKS
Lanham • Boulder • New York • London

Published by Lexington Books
An imprint of The Rowman & Littlefield Publishing Group, Inc.
4501 Forbes Boulevard, Suite 200, Lanham, Maryland 20706
www.rowman.com

Unit A, Whitacre Mews, 26-34 Stannary Street, London SE11 4AB

British Library Cataloguing in Publication Information Available

Library of Congress Cataloging-in-Publication Data

Library of Congress Cataloging-in-Publication Data Available

ISBN 978-0-7391-8343-4 (hardback: alk. paper)
ISBN 978-1-4985-1350-0 (pbk.: alk. paper)
ISBN 978-0-7391-8344-1 (ebook)

∞ ™ The paper used in this publication meets the minimum requirements of American National Standard for Information Sciences Permanence of Paper for Printed Library Materials, ANSI/NISO Z39.48-1992.

Printed in the United States of America

For Lorna,
With heartfelt gratitude for being by my side

My dearest Mikayla,
Let your sense of wonder and wisdom guide you always
in being the artist of your life

Contents

Preface

"Out of the tragedies of the past come the heartfelt hopes for the future, the resolve to make changes, and the power within to do so" (Kelm 1998, 178).

As a healer and as a bureaucrat, I have witnessed tragedies, such as self-destruction and painful, challenging times of crisis in some indigenous communities, as well as progress, in the form of healing and resilience. As there are many indigenous people engaged in healing from historical injustices, there are also many nonindigenous individuals who are beginning to decolonize, relearning history to better understand why many communities remain in crisis. Many indigenous people continue to be affected by the effects of colonialism, of trauma that has been transferred intergenerationally. Many indigenous people are actively engaged in redeveloping their communities through healing, cultural resurgence, and restoration. There is a reconnection to governance structures, to their indigenous languages, customs, and ceremonies. They are experiencing hope, and they hope to inspire other communities who remain in a state of learned helplessness and despair. As dismal as conditions appear at times in some indigenous communities, and as strained as relations can be between indigenous leadership and federal government officials, there is incremental progress, and it all begins with respectful dialogue. We, the settlers, owe it to the indigenous people to listen and learn from their loss, their resilience to survive, and their teachings.

I would like to say upfront that not all indigenous communities are in crisis, and unfortunately propaganda only profiles those communities who are struggling, and those that are in the healing process and are doing extremely well are rarely given airtime. When I refer to "indigenous people" I am actually referring to individuals I have met who identify with their cultural identity as indigenous, as Cree, Ojibwe, Mohawk, Innu, Inuit, or Métis.

My intention is not to reduce or exoticize their cultural identity. My hope is to not essentialize the voices of the individuals I have met and worked with. Also, it is important to note that what I share here in terms of disclosures and personal narratives are only those I have obtained consent for in terms of publishing or sharing their information or narratives. In addition, the views presented in this book are mine and not reflective of the Government of Canada. This book encapsulates my auto-ethnography. My intention here is similar to Paulette Regan (2005, 2010), a fellow nonindigenous woman working with indigenous people for over twenty-five years, like myself. I want to share my knowledge, my transformative experience and the invaluable life lessons I have received. These life lessons have propelled me to do more, to effect change. The more I listen, the more I learn, the greater my responsibility to engage in critical consciousness and reparative justice.

I am grateful for being able to work in a dynamic environment where I feel like I still can enable change. I am often approached by others who want to hear about my "job," and they respond by saying how great it is that I continue to empower indigenous people, and my response is always that I don't empower them as much as they empower me. My "job" does not feel like work when I connect with my purpose. My approach can be defined as moral, existential, and pragmatic. Daily I apply my old-fashioned work ethic that has been transferred to me by my grandparents and parents, which resonates with what philosophers and anthropologists refer to as Aristotelian virtue ethics, where "the 'being' of human life is not a set of qualities but rather processes of becoming, that is, its potentiality and its possibilities" (Mattingly 2012, 167). My advocacy is where my spirit belongs. I can say that I am doing what I want to do and that is to work with indigenous and nonindigenous peoples to learn from the past, build relationships founded on openness, dignity, and hope to better support healthy and sustainable community development. To my government colleagues I suggest you connect with your purpose and interest in nurturing change. To my fellow scholars, I hope my auto-ethnography triggers a feeling or thought whether it be unsettled or not, to inspire your own self-reflection, to connect with the power we have as knowledge builders and the impact it has on others. As scholars and social scientists with an abiding interest in indigenous peoples' past, present, and future, we are well placed not only to study history but to make it (Trevithick 1998). To my indigenous colleagues I ask that you continue to tap into your strengths, resilience, and faith that we will engage in mutual respect and collectively learn from each other and transfer this to the next generation.

My transformative learning has been and continues to be a cognitive, affective, and spiritual process, at times unsettling but always invaluable. My willingness to learn in a transformative way stems from my commitment to reconciliation. I cannot impose my ideas, feelings, or learnings onto others, but what I can do is share them. I hope to do just that with this book. A quote that has extreme relevance and resonance for me is from Carl Jung, also cited in Unni Wikan's work (2012, 31):

> Indeed, I do not forget that my voice is but one voice,
> My experience a mere drop in the sea,
> My knowledge no greater than the visual field in a microscope,
> My mind's eye a mirror that reflects a small corner of the world,
> And my ideas – a subjective confession

Welcome to my subjective confession, my story . . .

Acknowledgments

Sincere thanks, first and foremost, to Amy King from Lexington Books for approaching me and showing interest in my "story," for having more faith than I did initially in the potential of writing this auto-ethnography. I rarely walk away from such challenges, and so I am truly pleased I didn't walk away from this one. I want to thank the students I work with daily who have shown interest in my eclectic approach and who nurture me through their refreshing authenticity. As I tell them constantly, we have much to learn from students who remain connected to their sense of awe and wonder. I want to thank my colleagues, my dear friends, and my fellow scholars for their ongoing support and helpful critical feedback. To all my indigenous colleagues and friends, I thank you for your personal narratives and for your teachings—they have been more than enriching. And once again I want to thank Luke, the first indigenous individual I had ever met in my life and who happened to be my first child patient in art therapy back in 1989. He helped trigger my passion and my outrage at the injustices indigenous people faced, and continue to face. Luke also taught me that healing is founded on partnership. For the last twenty-five years, my thirst for human-to-human dialogue and partnership, my hope and faith in humanity, and my persistence and determination to effect transformative change continue to thrive. Every step toward such change was not in isolation but always in collaboration with indigenous people.

My journey has been defined through struggles, obstacles, loss, and pain. I have struggled greatly to "fit into" the mainstream. Now, my life experiences, my Elders' teachings, and my own wisdom have allowed me to follow my own stream. Coming home to where one is accepted is fundamental to all humanity, and it is the foundation to our well-being. Thank you Tom (a Cree bushman and patient of mine in the mid-1990s) for allowing me to showcase your artwork entitled "Coming Home" on the cover of this book. This image was so meaningful to him then and now resonates with me. I have been so fortunate to have met so many individuals who have impregnated my life and career with meaning. I remain forever grateful.

Wholehearted thanks go to my immediate and extended family and friends for accepting me, loving me, and supporting me. To my dad, my hero, for always believing in me and never questioning my spirit and for doing so without words, just meaningful, genuine gestures. To my mom, my precious caretaker, for always protecting me and worrying about my well-being and my sense of belongingness. To my big sister, for your honesty and sense of accountability and morality, those are great values I admire and always will. To my aunt Frances, thank you for providing me with that critical positive attitude that helped balance my core. To my grandparents, I miss you all so much it hurts, but my heart and soul are filled with memories that remain so alive, so real, and so fundamental to my being. Nana, I wish you were here to read this book!

Thank you to my precious daughter, Mikayla, for embracing me and my spirit. Thank you for your belief in me and your constant messages, "You got this mommy!" I hope that you continue to dance and connect with your own passion and gift to this world. My wish for you is that you pursue your dream with determination, sincerity, and compassion for others, and I promise your journey will be all the more meaningful.

To Lorna, thank you for encouraging me to write daily, and for providing me with critical and compassionate feedback on my personal narrative. And thank you for grounding me with your authenticity, nourishing my spirit with your heavenly, soulful voice, and allowing me to be me. With you, I truly feel at home . . .

Chapter One

Building Bridges

The "us versus them" dichotomous paradigm particularly with respect to Western-indigenous relations has always provoked my curiosity and frustration as to why it remains so prevalent, and my determination to deconstruct this dichotomy and create an intersection between the two poles. I am a Westerner, born and raised in Canada, living and breathing the values, traditions, and language of my Italian culture. My grandparents played a fundamental role in transferring our precious Italian dialect, in teaching me how to respect others and their cultural identities. Both my grandparents and my parents taught me through modelling what I refer to as my life values, framed by a heightened sense of humility. They always emphasized the value in learning from other cultures and languages through engagement with others. They felt they contributed to the country they call home and they always respected the fact that Italians along with other Europeans were settlers to a land already occupied by the First Peoples. My grandfather would often say, "Don't forget, this land is home for you because it was given to us by the Natives so treat them with respect." My grandparents were settlers, yet colonial ways of thinking were absent because they so valued and respected the fact that the opportunity for us to prosper in this country was thanks to the First Peoples. My grandparents embraced cultural diversity, different languages, customs, rituals, and beliefs. They were far from being Eurocentric; they were always eager to learn from others and then eager to share their experiences. They practiced the value of inclusiveness, and they showed me how to build common ground. Common ground is definitely built *not* found. So in my eyes, inspired by my grandparents' teachings, the dichotomy of us versus them is unnecessary, counterproductive, and only breeds more injustice. This dichotomy triggers my outrage and my passion to deconstruct it by practicing my values of respect for others through engagement with others.

1

At an early age, I wondered why distinct categories existed, categories that were made to be polar opposites. I asked myself "why should girls play with dolls and boys with cars?" I wanted to play with both and explore both realms, and thankfully, my mom allowed me. I brought the dolls to the cars and vice versa, much to the dismay of my friends, who appeared quite comfortable with nurturing the mainstream distinction of the two realms. I was fascinated by the bridge or intersection I created with these two distinct (or made to be distinct) worlds. I may have been exemplifying my androgynous side, but I was driven to create a place where I could choose to interweave two entities. This drive or unique lens came with a price; I was marginalized for being different, and I will describe this later in chapter 2. Nonetheless, this passion remains a fundamental characteristic of my core, an undercurrent that has defined my career path in many ways. I believe dichotomies are interwoven entities, juxtapositions that mirror each other. There is more to the words we use to create mutually exclusive categories or polarities, like body and mind, arts and sciences, us and them, verbal and nonverbal, left brain and right brain to name a few. Dichotomies are fluid and manifold (Desjarlais and Throop 2011), and there are synergies and interplays to be found between the two realms, and possibilities for dialectal relationships. In my view, creating dichotomous frameworks, such as top down versus bottom up, local versus global, centralized versus decentralized, is limiting and flawed, and they blind us from meaningful life experiences. There are meaningful relationships, interactions, and points of articulation that can be discovered. My passion to seek such meaningful intersections contributed to both my life experience of being "different," the challenges that come with it, and my enriching experiences as a healer and an advocate.

I chose art therapy as a career path because I had personally experienced the healing qualities of art making. For the longest time, I gravitated toward using art to express myself, to draw, paint, sculpt, and express my inner world, and give form to my emotions, my thoughts, and my life experiences. Art therapy made complete sense to me, and my belief and faith in the healing process made me a more effective therapist. When I completed my Masters in art therapy back in 1990, it was considered a unique profession, although not yet highly regarded by psychologists and psychiatrists. While talk therapy dominated the mainstream, art therapy was marginalized as it was generally viewed as an "artsy-fartsy," pseudo-type of helping profession. It was a challenge to prove the disbelievers wrong, but I embraced the challenge because during my internship with adult patients in a psychiatric ward, I witnessed the effectiveness of this treatment modality. Art therapy allowed me to bridge my belief in the healing qualities of art making and my interest in psychology and psychoanalysis. Polarities, such as verbal and nonverbal, dissipated once trust was established and an understanding formed that art therapy was a concrete and symbolic construction of space that allowed for the expression of the vicissitudes and contradictions of life that affect the individual. I also engaged in therapy myself to ensure I resolve my own issues and not transfer them onto my patients. I, like Sigmund Freud who coined the term "countertransference," believe that we can easily (most often unconsciously) transfer our issues onto our patients (Freud 1910). Many of my colleagues did not share my belief that a therapist should engage in self-analysis during one's clinical practice. Ongoing reflexivity has always been a key element in whatever I engage in because such practice adds value at a personal level, but also has meaningful repercussions onto my work and onto those I work with.

My first indigenous[1] patient as an art therapy intern at a residential treatment center was a nine-year-old Cree boy facing multiple challenges, such as aggressive tendencies, an attention deficit, sense of abandonment and fear, and extremely low self-esteem. Luke (a pseudonym) was also hearing impaired, and he refused to wear his hearing aid. He was experiencing marginalization even within the residential treatment center, as he was labelled at the center as "an *uncivilized child* who ate with his hands and refused to use utensils," as noted in his file. As an art therapy intern, I was asked to "create magic" and "transform" Luke. The racist attitudes of my colleagues at the center revealed to me that colonialism remained prevalent even in 1989. I recall feeling disgusted with their ethnocentric views, and I was quite vocal about it. I later found out that Luke's parents were traditional bush people and I was told they chose to live in the bush for six months of the year because they were driven to maintain their cultural ways and their language. They also expressed their concern with Luke refusing to wear his hearing aid as that was the main reason he was not allowed in the bush. Interestingly, as Luke was marginalized at the center, I was too as the art therapy intern. The child care workers often questioned the validity of this treatment approach. What was most important to me was that art therapy made sense to Luke and other patients I was seeing, and both my patients and I had faith in what I was offering. Luke was immediately drawn to me and the whole idea of engaging in the art-making process, and his preference was that we create artwork together. It felt natural and made complete sense to me to partner with Luke in his healing experience, to draw on the same page for his second drawing, and to engage in a dialogical process both verbally and nonverbally. Luke viewed his therapy as healing through partnering. I was reprimanded by my supervisor for following my instinct, as art therapy interns are discouraged to create artwork with their patients because we need to remain focused on the patient's experience and not get distracted by our own process. Nonetheless, I do not regret that I drew on the same page with Luke, listening carefully to his directives on what to do and how to draw. Although for subsequent sessions, I encouraged him to draw, paint, or sculpt on his own, but he would always return to his original request to create artwork together, and I think it is because he felt empowered in that first session where his request was acknowledged and respected. Through the art, the art-making process, our partnership in healing, an intersection of his world and mine was forged.

The bridging of indigenous insights in healing and partnering, with clinical insights led to a successful practice of sixteen years in art therapy, as a pioneer in cross-cultural art therapy with indigenous peoples, and it all began with Luke. In the end, a space was created, a refuge for self-expression and of possibility for cross-cultural dialogue and healing, based on humanity and respect (Ermine 2007). Art therapy with my indigenous patients became an interstitial space with its own distinct discourse, and a bridge between their reality and Euro-Canadian mainstream. Art therapy was reinterpreted by the Crees as "healing through art" (Ferrara 2004). As a Cree Elder told me, "in the Cree world, art and healing are part of life not separate from." At that given moment with Luke, although beyond my conscious awareness, my journey with indigenous people began, and it was founded on respect, partnership, collaboration, and readiness to engage in healing and reconciliation. I have listened to many narratives of personal lived realities, of our history told by indigenous individuals, survivors, children of survivors, living in remote, isolated communities, in the Arctic, sub-Arctic, as well as in some urban centers and those communities close to urban areas. I have been to over 200 First Nation and Inuit communities in Quebec, Ontario, and Manitoba. [2]

The healing experience was not only for Luke but for me as well, as it was the beginning of my personal journey to confront what my ancestors or the settlers had imposed on indigenous peoples of this land that I call home. I was ashamed and outraged of the Eurocentric knowledge I acquired in school about North American history; how the textbooks described the settlers' arrival to this land they discovered and how they "civilized the savages" and brought prosperity to all. The history I was taught invalidated the contributions of indigenous peoples, and I, like many Canadians, was not made aware of the cultural ethnocide they experienced. I was taught that the northern parts of Canada were "no man's land with no inhabitants," that "Indians" are a problem because they are all on welfare, depend on taxpayers, abuse their children, abuse alcohol and other substances, and many are homeless. I was never taught that "Indian" was a misnomer, nor was I taught that there was cultural diversity among the "Indians" of North America. I never knew until I started working with them that they were the first inhabitants of our land. The history textbooks I read always gave credit to Christopher Columbus discovering our land and whose mission was to civilize the savages they came in contact with. "Histories are stories we tell about the past," and I, like King (2012, 3), am disturbed by how certain stories are chosen over others and how those become the pulse of our history, like Columbus. Removing the indigenous voice from our history is a sad reality and a grave injustice. Those history textbooks were a tool used to promote Eurocentrism while oppressing indigenous peoples, which in the end fosters what I refer to as intergenerational colonialism, where both indigenous and nonindigenous peoples are deprived of their collective history.

In my work, I have learned and continue to learn from indigenous peoples, listening to their interpretations of history, their personal narratives, stories, and legends of their oral traditions. I have learned to appreciate the significant differences between indigenous and Western epistemologies, where indigenous epistemology is based on interconnected systems, holism, and experiential knowledge and what is important is considered immeasurable, Western epistemology is founded more on linear modelling and objective and positivist paradigms, defined by "if we can measure it, it is real."[3] Indigenous knowledge systems are highly complex, evolved, and holistic and can be interpreted as antithetical to Western positivistic science (Durie 2005). I have also learned that the more I engage in ground truthing, in connecting with indigenous peoples and see and hear about their lived experiences, the more I realize how Western knowledge systems can be limiting and need to be broadened in order to be more dynamic. I am currently witnessing a gradual cultural shift where indigenous knowledge systems are beginning to be recognized by Westerners as complex and with an adaptive integrity of their own. This shift is also fostering a growing appreciation of the complementarity that exists between what has been considered as two disparate and irreconcilable systems of thought (Barnhardt and Kawagley 2005), such as holistic treatment of certain open-mindedness, focus on interdependence of factors related to behaviors in humans, animals, and viewing nature as relationships. I have witnessed firsthand among indigenous peoples the value of oral tradition and on transferring communal narratives from one generation to the next. I can appreciate this cultural value as I have personally experienced it with my grandparents and my Italian heritage. The absence of this cultural tradition in indigenous and nonindigenous worlds would greatly compromise the continuity of knowledge and values. Although there appears to have been a neglect of narrative in the Western world (Ermine 2000), I think (and hope) that the paradigm shift will transform the neglect to recognition and value.

In my clinical work, I was criticized by my peers that I was only being introduced to a "slice" of indigenous reality. I accorded primacy to the "selves" I interacted with both within and beyond the clinical milieu, in various cultural settings, in their homes, bushcamp, and wigwams or teepees; to me, that was and still is more than just a "slice." I wanted to learn about past and current experiences of colonialism, I wanted to hear their lived narratives. The lived narratives have often reflected their cultural beliefs that have survived the effects of colonialism. And I was eager to visit their communities, experience their traditions, listen and learn from their distinct customs and languages. A fundamental belief that sits in my core is that indigenous peoples have a substantial and invaluable heritage from which we have much to learn. Both indigenous and nonindigenous peoples have lost significantly from the implications of colonialism and we, especially the nonindigenous people, need to confront the wrongs committed onto indigenous peoples and learn from the past. "We need to learn to listen differently" (Regan 2005, 2), learn from what we have *all* lost, learn from their resilience, and move forward with a readiness to reconcile, build meaningful relationships, work together to support sustainable communities, and coexist in a peaceful way.

An Ojibwe Elder I had met early on in my career shared his life experiences of trauma as a residential school survivor, how at eight years of age, he was literally pulled away from his mother's tight embrace, forcibly placed on a plane, and brought to a school "down south," far from his home community. He was physically and sexually abused by his teachers, nuns, and priests. He was told that his Ojibwe mother tongue was the "language of the devil," and they were going to get rid of the "savage" within him by "civilizing" him. He told me he was thankful he survived unlike many of his peers who died due to sickness and malnutrition, and who never had a chance to express their truth about how they were mistreated and abused in such inhumane ways. In his words: "I held onto my grandfather's words and stories of how our people welcomed the skinny, bearded white settlers, offering them food and shelter, showing them how to respect and live off the land and waters. They learned from us and us from them—we were respectful neighbors." He believed we can return to that peaceful coexistence because in his words, "it is something we had—we *can* return to something we have experienced."

Throughout my career, I have felt and continue to feel a gnawing sense of guilt that my ancestors were allowed to nurture their traditions, language, and culture and given the space to do so. I hold a privilege to have a space to express my language and cultural identity and at times, I do take it for granted. I cannot fathom not having this space. My core would be wounded if this space was taken away and if I was forced into a space that holds no meaning or value. And the fact that I have this space to be or sense of place and that my indigenous partners do not and that it was taken away and that they experienced cultural genocide in their own land, leaves me with intense outrage, guilt, and shame. I also feel anger at how colonialism remains prevalent in both explicit and implicit ways in how we treat indigenous peoples and how many still see them as inferior to nonindigenous people and as a burden to our society. This is perpetuated, I believe, by our inaccurate history education, and through myths and stereotypes reflecting Eurocentrism. Daily, I work on consciously transforming this guilt to reflection and social action. What fuels me is my outrage for the injustices indigenous peoples experienced and continue to experience, and my passion to educate nonindigenous peoples of this reality.

My ancestors were colonizers, and so daily I critically self-reflect and consciously try to ensure I don't impose paternalistic views, or my Western way of being onto my indigenous partners. Rather than deny my feelings of guilt and shame or remain complacent, I choose to transform these feelings. I cannot ignore them—I prefer to acknowledge, transform, and sublimate these emotions into action that is meaningful, effects change, and contributes to reconciliation. As noted by several nonindigenous scholars, it is of critical importance to continually reflect and interrogate our own colonial position that we have inherited (Regan 2010; Jones and Jenkins 2008; McCaslin and Breton 2008). In my eyes, the reason it is of such importance is because if not, I can easily retraumatize indigenous people and become the colonizer.

Early on in my career, while working in a Native Mental Health Research Unit, I was struck by how my fellow psychotherapists and psychiatrists were applying diagnoses to indigenous patients with little to no consideration of their cultural identity. The psychiatric constructs being used are clearly more relevant to and reflective of Western culture. I consider this a grave injustice. I channeled my frustration and rage by developing a research study where I examined the cultural differences in styles of emotional expressions by comparing Euro-Canadians and Crees. Some cultures, like the Crees predispose individuals to use nonverbal modes of emotional expression; however, this was then rarely considered in the clinical assessment and treatment processes. I challenged the assumption that psychiatric constructs and practices can always be appropriate cross-culturally. Even the current list of culture-bound syndromes perpetuates the racial bias in psychiatric diagnostic process and treatment. As Kleinman (1997) contends, disorders or constructs from non-Western cultures are referred to as "culture-bound," whereas the standard diagnoses are defined without any cultural qualification. When I presented the results of my research study in transcultural psychiatry (Ferrara 1999) to a group of psychiatrists, I was faced with resistance by many present, where one psychiatrist interrupted my presentation, openly denounced my work, and "advised" me to never question the validity of psychiatric diagnostic constructs. In his view, cross-cultural factors are irrelevant. I realized that more research was required to further explore cultural relativity in psychiatry. I also took pride in hitting a nerve and causing a wave that led to further debate and discussion. Moreover, in this research study, I was determined to prove that an "artsy fartsy" like me was capable of designing and implementing a qualitative and quantitative research study. It was personal accomplishment in bridging the infamous binary realms of arts and sciences and demonstrating that one realm informs the other.

DECOLONIZATION OF THE HUMAN SUBJECT

What I realized early on is that I can only control my own role in the reconciliation process, my own self-reflection, and my own healing. What I could offer the indigenous people I work with is heartfelt empathy for what they experienced, respect for their bravery and resilience, and my honesty and humanity. As a settler-ally (Regan 2010), this is how I contribute to the process of decolonization. In chapter 3, I will explore the settler in me as I believe, like Regan, that it is critical for me to acknowledge and to interrogate my own position as a beneficiary of colonial injustice. Because colonization wounded the human in the individual by denying them the space to be, decolonization necessitates rehumanization. Decolonization involves a paradigm shift from a culture of denial to the creation of space for indigenous cultural resurgence (Regan 2010), a space of shared humanity. Thus, my role and moral commitment in the rehumanization of indigenous people entails treating the individuals I meet with respect, and I honor and value my interactions, and the respect is reciprocated. Intersubjectivity and reflexivity permeates my everyday life and my work as I remain open to my sense of self and connecting with other "selves" in order to avoid turning people into objects (Salzman 2002, 807), and also, to pay close attention to individual lives as lived. I also believe it is critical to reflect on my relationship with the people I work with and it is not to indulge my narcissism but, as Bucholtz (2001, 181) argues, "To replace self-effacement in the research process with a heightened self-consciousness." Interestingly, many of my Cree informants asked that I include myself in my ethnography, and this request reminded me of Luke, my first Cree patient, and his request for me to create artwork with him. With all the anthropological research completed on Cree people, my informants unanimously felt that the works were devoid of truthful interactions between the anthropologist and the people they studied, and rarely showed how the anthropologist gained such knowledge. Most research they felt was divorced from the individual writing the ethnography, and so they encouraged me to include myself in my work. They clearly understood that I was offering an interpretation of their interpretations, a story about their stories of their life experiences (C. Geertz 1995), and a more humanistic ethnography, one that respected their voices and that held cultural resonance. Cultural resonance was predominant in the art therapy I provided, the research in transcultural psychiatry I led (Ferrara 1999), and the ethnography I created (Ferrara 2004), and remains in the foreground in the policy development I engage in. If my efforts do not evoke cultural resonance through our interactions and working relationships, then my efforts in decolonization are futile.

In chapter 5, I will further elaborate my contribution to the area of reflexive anthropology or humanistic ethnography, where the self of the informants and the ethnographer are not dormant. This book applies an auto-ethnographic methodology, where my own thoughts, feelings, and experiences shape my fieldwork and they are components of embodied research (Regan 2010, 30). As Regan (2010, 29) contends, "this approach is common in indigenous scholarship but still not as widely used in social sciences and history disciplines." Similar to Regan, my methodology involves using oral history evidence through my own storytelling, while documenting and analyzing my own lived experiences. Nevertheless, I believe we are seeing a paradigm shift in that social sciences in general, and anthropology in particular, are embracing the value of auto-ethnographic methodology and its contribution to humanistic ethnography. Personal narrative analysis is becoming more and more common in social sciences and viewed as a methodologically sound focal point (Maynes, Pierce, and Laslett 2008). My book also adds to the small number of policy makers who have written about their work with First Nations. Both Ciaccia (2000) and Penikett (2006) wrote about their experiences as bureaucrats working with First Nations and shared their personal insights. Both claim that Canadians need to better understand our colonial history, and both emphasize how reconciliation requires an open mind and spirit. Penikett (2006, 269) argues that "no treaty will ever be concluded until policy leaders—federal, provincial, and territorial—get personally involved." I had heard about John Ciaccia as the Minister of Native Affairs in Quebec and his peacemaking efforts during the Oka Crisis in 1990.[4] I never knew about how transformative the experience was for him until I read his personal account—how the crisis forced him to rethink his ethical responsibility, how he engaged in his own healing, and how the whole experience involved learning about history and human nature at an intellectual, physical, emotional, and spiritual level (Ciaccia 2000, 18). My hope is that this book will contribute to this invaluable domain of personal narrative analysis or auto-ethnography, accentuating the value of critical self-reflexivity.

In providing my indigenous patients with a space to express their notions of self, as a clinician and an anthropologist, I am contributing to the decolonization of the human subject. My research study (Ferrara 1999) contributed to decolonizing the Crees in that I challenged Western application of psychiatric diagnoses to Cree patients. I believe the continued application of such diagnostic tools without consideration of the patient's cultural identity promotes colonization through systemic assimilation, disempowerment, and marginalization. This research study continues to impact diagnostic processes with indigenous patients; my colleagues in psychiatry, psychotherapy, art therapy as well as my indigenous colleagues and community workers continue to reference it in their work and efforts in decolonization. It is not about being culturally sensitive toward indigenous people—it is more about being culturally competent, critically conscious, and compassionate. Simply put—to think, feel, and act with humble tenacity. Elders often thank me for my humanistic, compassionate ways, expressing their appreciation of my open spirit, giving them the space to be. This is my contribution to the decolonization and rehumanization, and this book challenges others to take action by critically reflecting on one's own assumptions and worldviews. This book may help propel the reader to consider how we promote the colonial legacy if we choose to do nothing, as complacency promotes colonialism (Regan 2010). It will hopefully percolate discussions within anthropology and the helping professions to rethink our relationships with our partners in the field and realize that self-reflection is not an option to consider but a necessary choice that rehumanizes the other and oneself, and restores and sustains human dignity. Evidence in the effectiveness of my approach will not necessarily be found in a vast number of scholarly journals but more from indigenous colleagues, Elders, community workers, youth leaders, and regional representatives who work on the front line. To me, this evidence or appreciation and understanding is fundamentally important as it validates my efforts toward decolonization.

My ethnography (Ferrara 2004) exemplifies an engagement with the Cree sense of space experienced in art therapy, a *space* that transformed to a *place* that is highly charged with symbolic significance due to their sense of self being embedded within it. In my clinical work, I did not apply a victim-centered approach to healing that pathologized indigenous peoples, which was a common approach among my colleagues in psychology and psychiatry. With every patient, I developed with the patient a treatment plan that spoke to both his/her weaknesses or issues and strengths or assets. For example, Luke, like many of my indigenous patients, felt disconnected to his cultural identity, yet he was able to identify an Elder in his life whom he reconnected with; the latter was considered a strength or asset to be tapped into to help rebuild one's identification with their cultural ways and language. Although more challenging within government, I try to apply a similar approach to policy development, as I will describe in chapter 4. Many policies that have been developed are reactive and crisis-oriented, and many continue to have a paternalistic undertone, such as the Western-based welfare system in place in many indigenous communities, suicide prevention, diabetes prevention programs rather than promotion of community-based economic development projects, and promotion of indigenous healing medicines and modalities. Also, in government, the silos we work in promote Western knowledge systems, and these divisions are apparent on the ground in communities, where the programs stemming from the siloed policies remain unintegrated. Therefore, in order to decolonize, we need to break down silos, challenge Western thinking, and consider if policies and programs are relevant or not to indigenous peoples. As policy developers, we need to realize that what we create has direct impact on the front line. The more integrated our policies, the more effective the programs once implemented on the ground. When we work in silos, we inadvertently create additional and unnecessary challenges for the people affected by policies. There have been more recent attempts to promote community-led and community-paced initiatives, such as community planning and First Nation–to–First Nation mentoring program. Such initiatives support the process of decolonization as they are strength based, community centered, and culturally meaningful.

In my personal evolution from art therapist, to healer, and then, to enabler and indigenous cultural activist, what has remained constant is how my efforts continue to contribute to the field of applied anthropology with the ambition and hope to deconstruct and demystify nonindigenous Canadians' perception of realities faced by indigenous peoples (Alfred 2005), and help transform the legacy of cultural oppression to one of cultural revitalization and restoration. Part of decolonization is to educate nonindigenous people of the effects of colonization, of policies that promoted the elimination of indigenous cultures. Acquiring knowledge of history, the experiences of colonialism, and how the effects are still being felt today in many First Nation, Inuit, and Métis communities contributes to decolonization and defines the role of nonindigenous people in the process of reconciliation (Regan 2005). As I will elaborate in chapters 6 and 7, reconciliation entails a sense of responsibility not for decisions made in the past but for knowing our history, learning from indigenous people, listening to their voices, and developing critical relationships that promote decolonization and cultural restoration. I cannot lead or direct cultural revitalization, but I feel it is my responsibility to support the movement by forging relationships, engaging in dialogue, being an external partner to help connect the dots in the maze of government policies and programs, and broker knowledge. My role is also to educate nonindigenous peoples, to transfer the knowledge I have obtained, help bridge the gaps, and demystify our recent history of indigenous and nonindigenous relations.

From Passive Recipients to Active Participants in Policy Development

After several years of clinical experience and a realization that I needed to enable change at a more global level, I accepted a position in the federal government at the department of Aboriginal Affairs and Northern Development Canada (formerly known as Indian and Northern Affairs Canada). I witnessed the effects of the legacy of colonialism, such as residential schools and forced assimilation, leading to intergenerational trauma,[5] a state of learned helplessness, and a sense of hopelessness in some communities. I worked in communities that faced profound tragedies, like an eight-year-old Ojibwe girl committing suicide. This suicide affected the whole community as well as the neighboring communities. Traumatic incidents like this have a significant ripple effect, oftentimes leaving individuals and communities in a state of paralysis and crisis. I once arrived at a remote northern community and noticed about 100 people lined up outside the nursing station. It was an extremely cold February day, and I thought they were waiting for personal supplies, such as food, clothing, and other necessities from the airplane I was on. When I entered the nursing station, the nurse rushed me to a room where a fourteen-year-old girl had just attempted suicide, and she was lying on a cot, connected to an intravenous to help remove the toxins from her body after she had overdosed. The nurse then told me the people waiting outside were waiting to see me. I was shocked. I had witnessed widespread community dysfunction, and the cause was colonization. Colonization led to trauma defined as destabilization, cultural shame, disempowerment, and isolation. I realized that day in February that I couldn't do this on my own, I couldn't heal the community. The sense of hope and the healing had to come from within the community. I realized that "collective dysfunction requires collective intervention" (Taylor and de la Sablonniere 2013, 22), so not only was it up to the community but government as well as it plays a role in providing the supports required and as defined by the community, *not* by government.

I have also witnessed the triumphs, the cultural resilience, an in-depth openness and understanding even after their experience of cultural ethnocide. In many communities, both as a clinician and government worker, I witnessed traditional ceremonies and longhouse rituals, feasts with traditional foods and dances to celebrate a new season, a birth, a wake, and a wedding. I also saw how some communities moved toward self-governance with a sustainable community plan in spite of the limitations of federal government programs and services. Government at all levels needs to move beyond the paternalistic, colonialist mind-set that undermines community development and well-being, and it needs to acknowledge their role in the past as well as the current situation many indigenous communities are in. We need to engage in the process of reconciliation with our indigenous partners rather than witness their healing process on the sidelines and then critique them for not effectively evolving and progressing.

Within the past eleven years in government, I continue to engage in decolonizing the human indigenous subject and promote cultural resonance in the development of policies. My efforts have been dedicated to including indigenous people in the development of policies that affect them and their well-being directly. By working closely with and learning from my indigenous partners as well as horizontally within my department and with other government departments, I have been actively promoting a place-based approach to policy development, where communities inform government what their priorities are and policies in turn are developed to reflect locally meaningful realities. This comes with its own challenges as it is difficult to promote a critical paradigm shift where bureaucracy needs to reconsider its ways and be informed by those at the grassroots level rather than impose top-down processes.

In a recent study on the quality of life in indigenous remote communities, we worked closely with a First Nation-run research organization and with six remote communities (five of which were First Nation and one Métis community), asking them to define their quality of life in these communities, and they suggested recommendations for further policy development. I invited all six community liaison workers to attend a think tank symposium in Ottawa to share their narratives of life in remote communities, as well as their definitions of what quality of life is to a large crowd of government officials. This led to the First Nation representatives partnering with government representatives, discovering existing programs they can tap into to help develop capacity within their communities to further develop youth programs, community gardens, etc. Although we have yet to implement all the recommendations from this study, we are actively voicing their concerns, ensuring we help create links with other government programs available and connect them with other First Nation communities that may act as mentors in community development. I will further elaborate on such place-based approach to policy development in chapter 4.

I am currently working on becoming a more effective enabler, knowledge broker, and facilitator of community-led development, community paced and community driven. I have developed and continue to form key partnerships so that I can contribute to the reconciliation process as the First Peoples of our nation heal and continue to nurture their cultural identities. I am continuously engaging with my partners, learning from them and integrating this knowledge into my own being, constantly reshaping, reforming, and refusing to remain static. This is akin to what Ermine (2007, 202) refers to as "the ethical space of engagement," which he believes is required in order to reconcile Western and indigenous worldviews. This "ethical space" is founded on human-to-human dialogue and self-reflexive practices, and it is what promotes reconciliation. I agree with Bar-Tal and Bennink (2004) who stress, ". . . it is only trust and respect that provide hope for better life and it is the duty of humanity to enable groups to follow the path of the reconciliation process. We, as social scientists, can contribute to a better understanding of this process and the factors that influence it. That is our mission to the well-being of human society" (30).

In 1989, I partnered with Luke in his healing journey, and now I partner with indigenous people from coast to coast to engage in dialogic exchange and provide support, tools, and knowledge requested and defined by them. In chapter 3, I will explore the evolution of my relationships, partnerships, and networks founded on a strong sense of trust. It is the right of all human beings to define, sustain, and perpetuate their identities as individuals, communities, and nations (Royal Commission on Aboriginal Peoples 1996), and so, whatever hat I may wear, whether it is art therapist, anthropologist, or enabler, one thing that remains constant is my advocacy and my profound affinity for indigenous peoples. I strongly feel it is my responsibility as a Canadian to help restore what was so wrongfully taken away, to give back to those who have enriched my being, and to present a narrative ethnography of the particular (Abu-Lughod 1991); that is, the particular voices I have had the privilege of listening to, interacting with, and most of all, learning from.

My daily impetus to effect change, to educate, to enlighten others emanates from a lived narrative of a former Ojibwe patient of mine, sixty-two-year-old Mary, who expressed her readiness one day to share her truth to me:

> I have a strong need to tell you what happened to me at residential school as a young child. I was stubborn and still am (she giggled). When I was spoken to by the very rude nuns in English, I would respond in my language (Ojibwe). They threatened me and I continued. I frustrated the hell out of them! One day the nun took a pair of scissors and told me that if I wouldn't speak English, God's language, she would cut my tongue. I responded in my language, '*You can take my tongue but not my voice.*' My tongue was cut often, I cried and cried but refused to let go of my language. I never shared this because I thought no one really cared. People need to know how many of us were abused. People need to know how some of us survived. Many of my friends weren't as lucky. They died and never said a thing 'cause they figured no one cares. Meegwetch . . . meegwetch [*thank you* in Ojibwe].
>
> Mary opened her arms to embrace me and then stayed there and cried, and cried some more.

This disclosure changed Mary's life as it gave her children a better understanding of why at times she was an absent mother, and why she abused alcohol in order to escape from her pain. Mary inspired others in her community to share their truths, their life stories. This is an important step in the healing process, which is contagious. From 1990 to 2005, many indigenous people came together, and they agreed to hold a truth commission. In 2009, the Truth and Reconciliation Commission of Canada (TRC) began to hold events across the nation to allow survivors to share their voices and experiences of trauma and resilience (James 2012). TRC is a grassroots approach, and for many indigenous people it is a key part of their healing process, and it is also a valid educational avenue for nonindigenous people. The stories are shared through the lens of trauma, hope, and healing through cultural resilience. There have been several related initiatives in Canada supporting reconciliation, such as Reconciliation Canada, a charitable project established as a collaboration between the Indian Residential School Survivor's Society and Tides Canada Initiatives Society, and the Reconciliation Week Vancouver 2013, where seventy thousand demonstrated their desire to deepen the dialogue and create a shared understanding toward a new way forward together

(R. Canada 2013). Like the TRC, these initiatives define reconcile as weaving a stronger and more vibrant social fabric, based on the unique and diverse strengths of Canadians and their communities (R. Canada 2013).

Inspirited by this same desire, I need to share how I have been empowered by the individuals I have met and those I continue to meet, interact with, and learn from. In the spirit and tradition of dialogue and storytelling, I present my narrative ethnography of the particular, my story and what I have learned and gained from other individual life stories. Undoubtedly, engaging in dialogue, sharing and listening to stories help us better understand each other and in the end, transform our identities (Neveu 2010). My wish is to remain faithful to my life story and to the lived narratives I have heard, and to acknowledge their intellectual, emotional, and spiritual sustenance.

NOTES

1. "Indigenous" and "Aboriginal" will be used interchangeably throughout the book. Essentially, both refer to the First Nations, Métis, and Inuit peoples of North America. My preference is the term "indigenous" because as many First Nations, Inuit, and Métis people have shared with me, it speaks to the relationship they have toward the land and the term "Aboriginal" is a term that was created by government. Nonetheless, "Aboriginal" has become so ingrained in many due to colonization that they apply it to describe their cultural identity.

2. Although I did work at several Urban Aboriginal centers, my focus here is more on my work in communities and less on Urban Aboriginals. I do respect the fact that Urban Aboriginal life is a unique reality (Alfred 2009, 50).

3. Source: *Sacred Ways of Life: Traditional Knowledge*. First Nations Centre, National Aboriginal Health Organization (2005).

4. The Oka Crisis was a seventy-eight-day standoff (from July 11 to September 26, 1990) in Kanesatake between Mohawk protesters, police, and the army. The proposed expansion of a golf course and the development of condominiums on disputed land that included a Mohawk sacred burial ground were at the heart of the crisis (York and Pindera 1999). While the golf course expansion was cancelled, the land claim by the Mohawks of Kanesatake has yet to be resolved. Overall, the crisis made more Canadians aware of indigenous rights and land claims; it also spoke to the potential for future conflict if such claims were not resolved in a timely, transparent, and just manner.

5. Intergenerational trauma is viewed as historical unresolved trauma due to a multigenerational legacy of colonization (Alfred 2009, 42).

Chapter Two

Being the Other

Throughout my career as a clinician and as a public servant, I have at times felt like I was "the other," the "untrusting whiteman," and rightly so. I was going into communities where many individuals were experiencing intergenerational trauma from the effects of residential schools, where a bureaucrat was viewed as an "Indian agent," who took children away from their parents. I had to prove myself, establish trust with my indigenous partners, patients, and coworkers. Sometimes it took longer than others, but in the end it was always worthwhile for both them and me. At one time, I had to visit this small, remote Cree community several times before being invited to go to the bushcamp for a goose break ritual, where geese are hunted and young boys enter manhood when they kill their first goose. Once the community members felt I was not a threat and that I was authentic in my interactions and in my desire to learn more about their cultural traditions, I was invited in. They also recognized that I would travel to remote communities, where some would take close to eighteen hours of air travel on small bush airplanes to get to if not more during the winter. Another experience I had was seeing a fourteen-year old girl, Rosie, in therapy for ten weeks, and she was angry and resistant, refused to talk or use the art-making process to express herself. She had experienced suicidal ideation, and she was placed in a treatment center, where she did not want to be. I would travel a two-hour flight every two weeks to see her and other Cree and Abenaki adolescents at this particular treatment center. At every session, I validated Rosie's silence and empathized with her anger. She would sit with her arms crossed, maintain a frown and she would stare down at me. I was getting anxious, and I wondered if I or art therapy was the best option for her. I was faced with the challenge of facing the mistrust and rebuilding. I decided to persevere and see where this would take us. At the third session, I asked if I could draw her, and she shrugged her shoulders expressing apparent nonchalance, yet she kept her eyes on the paper, showing some interest in my drawing. I drew Rosie for a few more sessions that followed and as a result, her body language gradually changed. At the eleventh week, she came in and I finally heard her voice, saying I didn't have to draw her because she wanted to talk. Rosie said she thought I was going to give up on her. She couldn't believe that I kept coming back to see her again and again. She then broke down, and expressed her traumatic life experience of being raped. At the end of the session, which lasted longer than usual, Rosie said she felt liberated and empowered. As she held onto the drawings I had made from the previous sessions, she expressed how the sense of trust we had established was so meaningful, and she especially appreciated that I validated her emotions, which was a first for her. "I have been so angry ever since that guy attacked me. I have been angry at everyone. I can't talk to my mom—she's always drinking and I have to take care of my small brother and baby sister. I just felt dirty and useless, and my anger at me and at the world just grew. Every time you came back, you allowed me to be angry, and you cared enough to draw me." She looked at me and just cried still holding onto the drawings. Rosie said she initially saw me as a white person who can never understand what her life has been like, and in her eyes, why would I care. By allowing her to be and in my acceptance of her silence, a safe place was created, and in the end, the whole experience was life changing for her. Rosie and her siblings went into foster care for a year while her mother sought treatment for her alcohol abuse. After a few years, I had heard that Rosie was back in her community living with her mom and siblings and actively involved in helping others with their healing.

I also consciously work at ensuring I am not treating "them" as the "other." I may have inadvertently done so while writing my research and ethnography but I recall focusing on developing my cultural sensitivity, being acutely aware of what I considered different and strange to me yet being sensitive to not define indigenous peoples as the "other" culture nor judge them through my own cultural biases. I worked on developing my communicative competence and understanding, interpreting, and applying specific discourse rules, such as appreciating long pauses of silence and that eye contact was not considered an important or valued feature in face-to-face communication. The development of one's communicative competence is an important prerequisite for ethnographic fieldwork (Jacobs-Huey 2002). I soon discovered the familiarity in the "strange." As Napier (1992) eloquently sets forth, "strangers within our midst are, indeed, the strangest of all—not because they are so alien, but because they are so close to us. . . . They cannot be completely exotic, for, were they so, we could not recognize them" (147). The static categories of "other" and "us" are not diametrically opposed nor are they homogenous; in my view, they both inform and through interaction define each other. As I evolve, I am realizing that there is more value in creating an ethical space, one of engagement based on human-to-human dialogue (Ermine 2007), without unnecessary distinctions between "me" or "us" and "them." Because as Gewertz and Errington (1991) note, "they" are related to "us"; their lives and our lives have significance for and influence on "them" and "us."

MARGINALIZATION

I feel it is important to share a fundamental aspect of my core self before moving forward. I have often been referred to as unorthodox, different yet unique, gifted, a genius, strangely straightforward, too open-minded, and too nonjudgmental (if that is even possible) to name a few, and I was slotted in these categories early on in my life. As mentioned in chapter 1, my life experience of marginalization began at an early age with my desire to bridge binary opposites. Another character trait I demonstrated at an early age was a powerfully heightened affect expressed through my altruistic ways, as I re-call always being driven by my desire to help others, and the gratification that followed affected my whole being. Family members, friends, and friends of friends were drawn to me for help when they were sad, sick, or just needed someone to talk to. It was not always a positive experience as I would often be misunderstood but it has been a defining trait, which was recognized and validated by a handful of people in my childhood, who were older and wiser; and in my adulthood, this has been recognized by my indigenous Elders. All defined this trait as my ancestral spirit. My psychologist defined it as an elevated level of intellectual and emotional intelligence.

Overall, I was categorized as different from the rest, especially my peers. Most of the time in my life, I felt like "the Other." During my elementary school years, my feelings of being misunderstood were quite intense especially amongst my peers and at school, at every elementary grade level, the teachers pushed that I skip a grade because I was not being stimulated by the curriculum. It was not until the fifth grade that my parents were convinced by my teachers, and I skipped sixth grade. Before actually skipping the grade, I had to undergo several psychological tests. The assessments labelled me as gifted, and unfortunately, skipping a grade did not really stimulate me as I ended up being further marginalized. Even my tendency to bridge dichotomies as discussed in chapter 1 and to balance negativity and positivity, which appears to annoy others at times, fosters my marginalization. It is especially annoying to those who prefer to feed the negativity and get further entangled in its web. In order to experience a sense of belongingness, I consciously (and most likely unconsciously) suppressed my "gift," "intelligence," and/or my "spirit" throughout my high school and university years. I would even catch myself as I got older to force myself to follow the mainstream and push my square peg into a round hole. Consequently, I feel I haven't reached my full potential because I suppressed it to such an extent all I have is a distant memory of the energy associated with the gift. Nonetheless, rather than feed the string of "I don't belong" that I experienced and create a paralyzing web, I decided to nurture my tenacity and resilience in hopes to inspire others to do the same. I have attempted to sublimate my "difference" especially through the professions I chose and not in a narcissistic way but in a way that would validate others as well as myself. Thankfully, my appetite for human interaction remains endless, and my natural instinct for inclusiveness remains intact. Admittedly, this is quite challenging to write about this life experience and more so about my gift, but what is driving me is my need to be transparent and human in expressing my vulnerability and my defining traits.

I feel that I can empathize with others with a level of understanding that would be absent or diminished if I had not experienced such marginalization. I am not saying that I experienced anything remotely similar to the cultural genocide and forced assimilation of indigenous peoples in North America. All I am trying to convey is that I can empathize with the experience of marginalization and what I can relate to is the need to connect with a sense of belongingness, and how sharing my story and listening to others sustain my sense of connectedness. I understand how marginalized people derive meaning from narratives as I do too, as narratives always begin as conversations and then develop into genuine dialogue that holds value, energizing both the speaker and the listener. I have experienced narratives or stories told in the context of advocacy or consciousness raising or mutual help, which entails the kind of empathy that matters morally (Cruickshank 1997; Antze 2010). And I applied this profound sense of empathy and my powerfully heightened affect as a therapist working in First Nation, Métis, and Inuit communities, and I continue to apply it through my work as an applied anthropologist. Lennon (1995) argues that it is important for people to reflexively engage with marginalized peoples and knowledge to become aware of our own experiences. This requires using critical discursive practices of learning and synthesizing new information, including different worldviews and paradigms from our own. Reflexivity is not simply about learning about the other but understanding the perspective from which a person sees the world and both parties engaging subjectively in that process (Lennon 1995). Becoming a partner within the reconciliation process involves this type of reflexivity as well as empathy. Reconciliation involves learning from each other, integrating the knowledge into one's being, and constantly evolving, reflecting, and not remaining static (Laughton 2012), but fully engaged in the relationship-building process.

ART THERAPY AND ANTHROPOLOGY—THE UNDERDOGS

Interestingly, the professions (i.e., art therapy and anthropology) I chose are themselves in some ways marginalized in Western society. Art therapy has gained recognition in the last twenty years as a credible profession. When I first started, it was not viewed as equally valid to talk therapy—it was clearly marginalized in the field of psychology, and perhaps it still is devalued and unknown for some helping professionals and medical doctors; nonetheless, it continues to grow as a viable treatment modality with children and adults. Art therapy is different from the mainstream talk therapy because it offers the option of self-expression through the art-making process. My approach in art therapy was patient centered, and I would assess each patient's readiness as well as evaluate if art therapy was the best treatment modality to address their needs. With my nonindigenous patients, I would often be faced with initial resistance and some fear of this "unknown" form of therapy, and so I would have to demystify art therapy and let patients know they did not necessarily have to be artistic to be an art therapy patient, just willing to use the art supplies as they deemed appropriate. With my indigenous patients, art therapy made complete sense to them, and it was rarely if not at all questioned as a healing approach. To my surprise and with such ease, I became a pioneer in cross-cultural art therapy with indigenous peoples, where my work with Luke had such a ripple effect as it led from one referral to another (Ferrara 2004). Many of my patients would still engage in "talk therapy," as they would openly express their thoughts and feelings while engaged in the art-making process or talk about their self-expressions afterward. In my experience, rather than distinguishing the two types of modalities—that is, art therapy and talk therapy—they were quite integrated, and the integration was integral to the healing process as defined by my patient's particular needs and aspirations.

I chose anthropology in my graduate studies because I viewed it as a field where I can nurture my thirst for deconstructing cultural phenomena and understanding how humans interpret and experience their cultural identity, especially as it was being highlighted as a salient feature within my indigenous patients' treatment plans. I was driven to explore the underpinnings of colonialism and how one culture can dominate and marginalize other cultures. I was also fascinated in the postmodernist movement that rejected anthropology as a science because anthropology unlike science is in the business of discovering meanings, and that meanings are derived from culture and thus are incommensurable (Spiro 1996; cf. Rosaldo 1989). Anthropology was clearly in an identity crisis defined by a dichotomous struggle, where it was trying to gain validity as a social science discipline while it advocated for the voices found in both Western and non-Western cultures. Similarly, both art therapy and anthropology were struggling to form their identities, although the latter was an older discipline. I was determined to contribute to both these seemingly "underdog" disciplines experiencing at times painful growth spurts, which in the end will only add to their value and potential.

For many decades, anthropology presented itself as a science dominated by the objectivist paradigm where it was believed that the anthropologist can write about the culture or field without locating his or her position in that world. As a social science discipline, anthropology has always embodied social movements (Ortner 1984). Because anthropology evolved alongside colonialism, cultural oppression defined the anthropology agenda, which led to the development of critical anthropology, aimed at critiquing oppression of Western culture onto non-Western cultures. The ethnographer's goal was to explore the resistance of non-Western and marginalized peoples (D'Andrade 2000), and consequently, moral advocates emerged. As D'Andrade (2000) argues, if moral advocates do good work that supports their moral agenda, then such work complements and enhances the quality of this social science. "Such work, whatever its animus, because it advances knowledge, helps rather than threatens the scientific agenda" (227). Anthropology has always been considered as a unique social science given the ethnographic fieldwork involved and the challenge of translating one's experiences and applying theoretical frameworks, resulting in an ethnographic product. Anthropology has faced the challenge of defining itself and its unique position in bridging scientific and humanistic inquiry. Ethnographic field notes can be viewed as scientific data and as interpretive text. However, this has also nurtured its identity crisis, which I believe was caused by the creation of a false dichotomy between science and the art of interpretation. I also do not think that cultural anthropology has gone through a "radical despecialization" (D'Andrade 2000). Anthropology may be considered an uncomfortable science to some given the critical social issues and deep ethical concerns from which there is no escape (Wikan 2012), but I think it is these unique attributes that makes it a rich discipline. I believe anthropology, along with its subdisciplines like medical anthropology, psychological anthropology, continues to evolve with the times as an invaluable and solid discipline because of its unique, continuing practice of ethnography. What enriches the discipline is ethnographies wherein research subjects as well as the researcher are not alienated and the principles of transparency and translatability are applied (Jacobs-Huey 2002). Anthropology cannot be forced into a single shared scientific paradigm because of its eclectic nature, which fosters varied forms of discourse.[1] Much like in art therapy where critics argue that the interpretive process of the art created is subjective and therefore not "valid," ethnographic field notes reflect the bias of the researcher (Appell 1992) and thus are not objective enough to be considered scientific. This perception contributes to anthropology not being as credible as other social science disciplines. My view is that both anthropology and art therapy have great potential to contribute to the betterment of humanity, each with their own distinctive approach, yet common in both is that the point of reference is grounded in dialogue and interactive relationships. What is missing in these critiques is the emphasis on the value of the discourse, the relationship, and the experiential knowledge, which has meaning for the patient and therapist, as well as the informant and anthropologist.

BECOMING A PUBLIC SERVANT

I am often asked why I left my clinical practice of sixteen years. I have always had a passion and drive to do more. My indigenous colleagues as well as my university students also encouraged me to take this position in government. The main reason I accepted this government position is to effect change at a more macro level using my knowledge base that I acquired at the community and individual level. My becoming a public servant encouraged me to apply anthropological theories to my daily operations and activities. Much of the techniques or approaches I used as a clinician were translated into my work as a public servant. My patient-centered approach led to promoting a community-centered focus in policy development. This does not come without its challenges. As mentioned earlier, one challenge is the bureaucratic system I work within and how paternalistic it can still be. However, there have been recent developments that are indicative of efforts toward reconciliation. On occasion, another challenge I am faced with is the sense of mistrust in some indigenous stakeholders. They have reason to not trust the bureaucrats who have caused the grave social conditions they live through daily as a result of colonialism. Most of the indigenous partners I work with do consider me as one of the few compassionate bureaucrats. One First Nation man told me recently that he is pleased to see that there are some bureaucrats who are willing to be part of the solution, as they need to accept the reality that they are part of the system that created the problems in the first place. As public servants, we need to learn to listen, engage in interpersonal understanding and introspection, anchored in an awareness of history and indigenous aspirations (James 2012).

When I first started my job in the federal government, I was immediately made to feel like a distant other as I was not a "common bureaucrat" given my clinical experience. I was told on my first day that my doctorate meant nothing compared to years of experience in the public service. Another reality that contributed to my marginalization was my telework arrangement. I was the only one in the department then who was working from home. It was offered to me, but everyone I would meet in government thought I had asked for it. I would often hear that teleworking was ineffective in the policy world, or that the best discussions are around the water cooler in the office, and so, in their eyes, I was missing out. For me, this arrangement further accentuated my self-discipline as I applied my strong work ethic to make this work. I was in constant contact with colleagues and stakeholders, and after ten years of teleworking, my reputation of being accessible, effective, reliable, and productive only heightened. This was quite the personal challenge, which I felt I overcame.[2] Interestingly, in terms of my clinical background, only a handful of fellow bureaucrats have shown interest in hearing about it except for the students who work with me. During my first year in government, I was invited by a First Nation colleague to present at a conference on Aboriginal research and policy and asked to launch my second book, which had just been published. Only one of my nonindigenous colleagues attended to show her support. I soon realized that my academic background and my years of experience in the field were viewed as a threat and so it was easier to either denounce it or not recognize it at all. Admittedly, the first few years in government were quite challenging and at times depressing, but that was when I sought my Elders and their wisdom and support to keep nurturing my mission and my raison d'être. I was told by one Inuit Elder, Angaangaq whom I called Uncle,[3] that this was going to be one of my life's great challenges and so I needed to tap into my spirit and my patience while dealing with others' complacency and especially with their fear of change. In Uncle's words, "Just stay connected to your spirit by listening to your heart, to follow its beat, and that the beat of a drum is there to remind us to do just that. Don't give up on your spirit's immense mission." Uncle Angaangaq's most powerful insight that he shared with me and others was: "The greatest distance in the existence of man is not from there to here or here to there. The greatest distance in the existence of man is from his mind to his heart. Unless you conquer that distance you will never learn to soar like an eagle, to realize your own immensity within."

Another interesting experience is that where my indigenous partners appreciate my compassion, many of my fellow bureaucrats question it because it is so foreign and unfamiliar. Although most bureaucrats complain about the missing human factor in bureaucracy and the lack of compassion and sincerity, at the same time they question why I care so much, why am I so considerate of others. For instance, a remote community had experienced an emergency once, and so one of the members of the community had emailed me informing me of the devastation they were experiencing. I immediately followed through the emergency procedures to ensure the supports were in place for this community of 150 people. Thinking I had followed the department's protocol (and I did), I was questioned by my then supervisor as to why I had "the need to save them." I wondered to myself, if we are here in government to enable and support community development, then how do we go about doing that without compassion? Thankfully, I decided to not suppress my compassion and sincerity because of this experience, and continue to follow my instinct and the guidance of my First Nation colleagues, who appreciate it. Interestingly, the day after, the superior official had thanked me for going beyond my call of duty, and so I was comforted by the fact that there are other bureaucrats with a sense of humanity.

When I left my clinical practice, some of my First Nation partners teased me for going to work on "the other side," but they understood my mission was to ensure that their voice was heard by bureaucrats who are detached from their lived realities. I work in the federal government department that led the residential school legacy, along with the Catholic, Anglican, Methodist, United, and Presbyterian churches. For more than 100 years, from 1857 to 1996, "Indian Agents" were employed by the Department of Indian Affairs to forcibly remove children from their families and communities, and place them in residential schools, where the missionaries forcibly through assimilation eradicated "the Indian" in the child (Miller 1996). In a comprehensive account based on extensive research, including interviews with residential school survivors, Miller (1996) claims that the motives of the First Nations peoples in obtaining an education were more authentic than those of the government and the churches. He places the major blame on both the government and the Canadian people as what was the "sin of interference" then, has now been replaced by the "sin of indifference" (Miller 1996, 435). Therefore, there is a legitimate, deep mistrust indigenous people possess toward government, especially toward the department I work in. As a government official, I have visited many communities, including small and very remote communities, and I have encountered the mistrust firsthand, and so, I had to validate their mistrust, re-establish their trust, and rebuild. Such experiences reminded me of when I first visited a Cree community in northern Quebec as a clinician, and two Cree women picked me up at the airport and asked me to sit in the back of the van. For a three-and-a-half-hour ride, I sat next to a dead beaver, whose eyes were glaring at me, and the Cree women giggled during the whole time. I was told I was being tested to see if I could handle it. I admit it, it wasn't easy, but I respected the fact that had to introduce me to their cultural ways in a "subtle" fashion. After I passed that test, I was introduced to hunting in the bush on my next visit! When I first started working in indigenous communities, I immediately experienced a sense of safety and humility. As much as I was exposed to cultural experiences and beliefs different from my own, the strange soon became familiar, and I felt safe. I experienced a sense of place where I was allowed to be me. No labels, no categories, just simple acceptance and faith in what I had to offer. I adapted to fit the local conditions and expectations, and I showed my ability to communicate in a way that earned their respect and trust. Moreover, I was overcome and overwhelmed with their unconditional generosity, and I feel to this day that I can only hope to reciprocate by making their voice heard. When word had spread quickly from one community to another, from southern to northern Quebec and then Ontario and Manitoba, about the effectiveness of the art therapy I provided, a Cree social worker told me: "When we believe in something, it spreads quickly from one community to the next, just like we did in the past when we shared medicines, hunting practices that worked." One Elder told me that I was considered as a member of their community, always welcomed and respected. In the same breath, she encouraged to not forget who I was, and to remain connected to my own cultural identity. These words of wisdom still intrigue me as they came from a woman who experienced forced assimilation through residential schools. What this advice speaks to is her resilience as it was her connection to her own cultural identity that sustained her. I experienced firsthand, through individuals like this woman and many others with an indigenous cultural identity, that "cultures that have been shown historically to be the most open to the outside are also those that are the longest-lived" (Napier 1992, 147). For many indigenous communities, the openness "to the outside" unfortunately led to their experience of cultural oppression but for many, it forced them to be even more resilient or fight for their existence through sustaining their cultural resilience. Many indigenous cultures in North America were oppressed and denigrated through attempts of forced assimilation, and many have survived because of their resilience and valiant efforts in cultural revitalization.

With such wise words of advice, this Elder showed her openness as well as her integrity and respect for me and my life experiences. These words continue to guide me because remaining connected to my cultural identity can only strengthen my cultural competence. She simply advised me to not deny my sense of identity in my mission to help others. My personal life experiences of being marginalized and in being the other have affected my lens, my reality and at the same time they fuel my drive to make a difference, to share narratives of individual lives as well as that of my own, to educate and enlighten others as well as to evoke sameness or a sense of connectedness. As an applied anthropologist, engaged in humanistic anthropology, I too believe that "we must with passion—at times, with outrage—convey, as best we can, complexities of life that both differ from and articulate with our own" (Gewertz and Errington 1991, 89).

NOTES

1. It is its eclectic nature that attracted me to the field of anthropology. Due to my cross-disciplinary approach (often perceived as "eclectic"), it can be a challenge to be recognized solely in one field. Interestingly, my nomadic journey along with its integrative elements has never been questioned by my indigenous partners. Although this is becoming more common, I often get questioned as to which profession I hang my hat on, and my answer is: neither, as I consider myself an advocate. These professions were and are avenues to channel my passion, which can be simply defined as advocacy.

2. After nine years as a government teleworker, I was asked to present on teleworking as a best practice at a conference on greening government operations.

3. Uncle's real name is Angaangaq Angakkorsuaq, and he is a shaman, healer, storyteller, and carrier of the qilaut (wind drum). He is an Inuit-Kalaallit Elder whose family belongs to the traditional healers of the Far North from Kalaallit Nunaat, Greenland. His name means "The Man who looks like his Uncle" and so he asks to be referred to as Uncle. When I had the honor of meeting Uncle in the early 1990s, he was already known to bridge the boundaries of cultures and faiths in people young and old. Since then, he has brought his teachings around the world, including South Africa, North America, South America, Asia, Arctic Europe, Russia, and Siberia. Uncle Angaangaq conducts healing circles, intensives, and Aalaartiviit, traditional sweat lodges. His teachings are deeply rooted in the wisdom of the oral healing traditions of his people. In 2004, his family summoned him to the sacred mountain for his initiation as their shaman (Wisdom 2011).

Chapter Three

Rebuilding Trust through Dialogic Exchange

One former chief of a First Nation community told me that the only way to move forward and heal from the wounds of colonialism is to rebuild the relationship between indigenous and nonindigenous peoples. This entails rebuilding a sense of trust, acknowledging the wrongs of the past and learning from them, and focusing on the healing process, and supporting prosperous and sustainable indigenous communities that contribute to the overall prosperity of Canada. This also entails educating the Canadian population of the lived realities of indigenous peoples and broadening their perspective, demystifying the stereotypes, and learning from each other through dialogic exchange.

Dialogic exchange leads to intersections of knowledge and discourse, which results in codeterminative processes in place of dichotomies. The dialogic exchange that I have experienced involved the interweaving of the verbal and nonverbal levels of communication. As an art therapist, the art-making, interpretive, and self-reflective processes, as well as the relationship were defined by the intersection of verbal and nonverbal processes. As an anthropologist and my experience in cultural bridging, the dialogic exchange also bridged the verbal and nonverbal realms creating a unique discursive form, based on the vicissitudes of the connection and interaction between my cultural identity and those of the individuals I worked closely with. To illustrate further, I will describe my first experience in a northern Inuit community. Soon after I arrived in this community located in the Arctic, I was invited into the home of the director of social work, an Inuit woman, whom I will refer to as Susan, who had picked me up at the airport. It was a cold day in January and as soon as I walked in, I noticed winter boots and clothing spread across the floor. I was careful to not step on anything. Kids were playing basketball in the narrow hallway, and as soon I entered the kitchen I noticed a large, dead, skinned caribou lying on the kitchen counter and hanging off one end because the counter was not large enough. I recall being in a natural state of shock, having never been this close to a caribou let alone seeing it lying on a kitchen counter. Susan asked me if I would like to join them for a caribou steak lunch. She glanced at me after she asked, and I am sure she noticed my discomfort. As I continued to scan the room, I also noticed a large polar bear skin hanging on the wall, leaving me in awe, which transformed to curiosity. I realized I had not yet responded to Susan, but she was not gesturing or demonstrating any body language that would indicate her frustration with the long pause I needed to process and embrace this new experience. Susan allowed me the time I needed to absorb and process this different cultural experience, and I remained so thankful for that time granted to me in such a respectful way. I experienced how silence is valued as a means for increasing understanding of oneself and one's environment (Carbaugh 1999), which is a common cultural value among the Inuit and many First Nations. It was not forced onto me, which is what I am used to being of Italian origin; she did not try to fill in the gap of silence, again what I am used to, as the silence was understood as a necessary element of my experience of acculturation. Her recognition, respect, and empathy enriched my experience and most likely added flavor to the best steak I ever ate in my life!

During one of my first experiences in the bush, I witnessed a dialogic exchange between an animal and a hunter, and I learned how an animal has to show its readiness to be hunted and to grant its natural gift to humans in its death. In another of my most uncomfortable yet fascinating life experiences, I walked closely beside a Cree hunter, Sam, who was hunting for rabbits on that particular day. As we walked, I paid close attention to mimic his hunting protocol, which was to walk a few steps and then stop and walk a few more and scan the environment looking for rabbits. I remained silent, but I was crippled with fear as I had no clue what was going to happen next, and I feared hearing the first gunshot and witnessing a rabbit die. Suddenly, a rabbit came right before us, about ten feet away and stared into Sam's eyes, and I shook like the leaves that surrounded me, thinking "I can't do this, I can't watch, I'm sick to my stomach." The rabbit left, and I stood there still shaking yet relieved. Sam empathized with me, smiled, and said: "He [the rabbit] told me he was not ready to give me his gift of life. When he is ready, he will return." There was a dialogic exchange between the rabbit and the hunter, one that the hunter referred to as common sense.[1] I witnessed a metacommunication between an animal and a human engaged in a relationship with an element of trust. There was a connection from one being to another, understood by the animal and the hunter. My discomfort and fear was balanced with intrigue and determination to learn more about a cosmology I was faced with that was different from my own, and Sam showed me the same respect as Susan did and that was to take the time I needed to embrace what was unknown to me. As Carbaugh (1999, 260) describes, I also became acutely aware of "my own habitual ways focused as they often are to hear the human over the animal, the individual person above the activities of the place, the linguistic thought over the audible nonverbal." On that particular day in the bush, I was enriched with experiential knowledge that transformed me, and I remain grateful for it. This was more than an adventure, and it satisfied more than my intellectual curiosity—it held a spiritual value for me. I took the risk to share my vulnerable side in going to a place foreign to me, and they reciprocated by taking the risk to bring me to this place. My readiness to learn and feel unsettled was recognized and respected. I went to a place of not knowing, which is conducive to learning that engages my whole being, including my spirit (Regan 2005). Such "moments of freely given trust" (Mahmood 2002, 2), and I would add respect, nurtured my transformative process as an individual, a therapist, and an anthropologist, as well as my commitment to working and learning from my indigenous partners. Several of my Cree patients would refer back to their bush experiences and relationships to animals and so, having experienced with my own eyes the strong connection between man and animal, enriched my understanding and therefore enhanced my effectiveness as a clinician. I was more knowledgeable in my interpretive process when artwork my patients would create symbolized their relationships to animals (Ferrara 2004).

As a public servant, the bridging remains quite present; however, my role now is more of a bridge builder and knowledge broker as I apply the lessons of my past experience and educate others on how to engage in the bridging process, learn from each other, build relationships with the intent to re-establish networks of trust, leading to reconciliation. The dialogue, the exchange, whether in the clinical milieu, in the field, or in my current government position, entails a dialogical awareness of one's self and of the other you are engaging with. The goal, as I see it, is to attain an intersubjective understanding. As Clifford (1989, 562) eloquently writes, "the point of dialogical awareness is to decentre the self, to focus neither on the (intimate) self, nor on the (distanced) other but on the historically and politically constituted field of relationships *between* (and constituting) self and other" (author's emphasis).

MISTRUST AND APPREHENSION

The relationship between indigenous and nonindigenous people is historically and politically constituted. Many First Nation, Inuit, Métis people today remain distrustful and angry at government for having created the dismal situation they face. They were forced onto reservations by the federal government's assimilation policies, isolated from other communities and fellow Canadians, treated like uncivilized savages, and forced into residential schools from the late 1800s up until 1996. This history is quite recent. In the 1960s, indigenous children were removed from their homes and placed in foster care at an alarming rate (Ross 2014). This was clearly another instrument of colonization, and it was not coincidental, as Ross (2014) claims. Johnston (1983), a researcher for the Canadian Council on Social Development, coined the term the "sixties' scoop" to describe this period from the 1960s to late 1980s where an unusually high number of indigenous children were apprehended from their homes and they were either fostered or adopted by nonindigenous families.[2] The cultural oppression they experienced and the disconnection to their cultural identities, their language, and their cultural ways have led to the high suicide rates, unemployment rates, violence, sexual abuse, substance abuse, poor health, and mental illness prevalent in many communities that remain in crisis and in a state of dependency on government programs, which nurtures a sense of powerlessness (Kirmayer, Brass, et al. 2007; Kirmayer, Simpson, and Cargo 2003). Many have internalized what they were taught in residential schools and how they were oppressed, discriminated and traumatized, and made to feel inferior. As a result, these feelings of despair and learned helplessness have been transferred onto the next generations. Given that residential school and the sixties' scoop survivors were taken away from their parents, families, and communities, they did not experience being parented, loved, or wanted, and instead they were oppressed and many times abused. Therefore, many learned to do the same to their children.

As one survivor who was accused of being a sexual abuse perpetrator in his community said after his court sentence: "That's all I know. I don't know how to be a loving parent—I was five years old when I lost my parents and went to school down south. When I came back, I was sixteen, lost and confused and then I started drinking to escape the bad memories. I treated young kids like I was treated by the priests. I abused my daughter 'cause that's all I know [crying]." His daughter, Maddy, remembered being abused at fifteen months old until nine years old when she broke down, disclosed the abuse but no one believed her, and then attempted suicide. She was placed in a mental health care facility, where she was referred to me for art therapy. After the first few sessions, where she was just crippled with fear, she decided to draw when she felt safe. Her pencil drawings were the most descriptive I had ever seen. The more I validated her artwork, the more she drew. Maddy's drawings depicted her experiences of being abused, sexually and physically, of how her father would leave her in a truck, unheated in freezing cold temperatures. She disclosed every detail verbally and through her artwork and cried. Consequently, her father was arrested, and I became her advocate in court, where the judge based his ruling on her disclosures, including her artwork, and sentenced her father to prison. Maddy was ostracized in her home community, where no one believed her and felt she fabricated the whole story; this community happened to be in a state of extreme crisis. One of her relatives in a neighboring community took her into their home, and Maddy returned to school, and later became a youth ambassador. The last time I saw Maddy, who was then fifteen years old, she told me: "I can never forget what my father did to me, but I had to get out of that mess or I was going to do the same." She established a strong relationship with an Elder who taught Maddy her native Ojibwe language, knowledge, and cultural traditions, which she said helped her heal along with the treatment she received. As a clinician, my primary goal was to develop a rapport leading to a relationship, a dialogic exchange founded on a sense of trust. I needed to understand this profound mistrust toward government, but given that I was going into the communities as a helping professional, it did not take a lot of time to establish a sense of trust, although at times I did experience resistance, but through ongoing presence and acknowledgment of this historically constituted mistrust on my part, I was accepted. In the early years of my career, I was often tested by community members to see if I was ready to be immersed in their cultural rituals, food, and ceremonies. In the end, they were testing my integrity and rightfully so. The communities I worked in were constantly invaded by outsiders, researchers, clinicians, anthropologists, nurses, doctors, etc. I have always dedicated time to understand every community I visit or work in for a long period and to engage in grassroots relationships (Turner 2006).

In one First Nation community where the crisis was heightened, I even passed armed gunmen because they knew I was going in to work and treat children in schools and Elders in the hospital. When I would fly to remote communities, many in the sub-Arctic region, I was always welcomed. Nonetheless, in several communities I was faced with violent conditions, where alcohol and substance abuse were rampant, children and teens would sniff gas, hairspray, and white-out and even drink cologne and mouthwash. At times, I had to sleep with a knife under my pillow. I knew I was considered by some as the whiteman-outsider and that I was only living there temporarily while holding my clinics. I was surrounded by lateral violence in these communities where the oppressors oppress themselves as well as others. As a result of colonialism and having experienced cultural oppression, many indigenous individuals feel powerless, and so they displace their anger toward their fellow community members. Lateral violence is often considered a repercussion of intergenerational or historical trauma (Bombay, Matheson, and Anisman 2013; Bombay, Matheson, and Anisman 2011; Alfred 2009). Part of the colonized mindset is the self-hatred, which can be internalized and self-directed or externalized and directed towards others (Alfred 2009). The violent conditions I witnessed were particularly found in communities that were in a state of paralysis, a state of extreme crisis, not yet ready to engage in the healing process; however, there were pockets of individuals and families seeking help in these communities in crisis. Such conditions made me fearful at times for my safety, but it never destabilized me as I understood the root causes of the despair, helplessness, accumulated loss, and shame these individuals are experiencing. I also have a strong support system in place that I draw from as needed when I experience vicarious trauma. [3]

As a therapist, I witnessed the trauma firsthand in many individuals, and for those who were ready to engage in healing, together we built trust in what I was offering, they had faith in the process as art therapy or healing through art resonated with them. While I was holding a clinic in a northern community, I had noticed an Anishinaabe Elder sitting in the waiting room, and so I assumed she was waiting to see someone. She returned a few days in a row and sat there quietly, so I approached her curious to know who she was waiting for, as I noticed that she was not being seen by anyone nor did she accompany any of the patients who were coming to the nursing station. I introduced myself, and she immediately responded saying, "I know who you are, I heard about you. You can call me Nookmis, grandmother in Anishinaabe." She shared her concerns with the youth and her community and how they were disengaged with their language and culture. Even though they were experiencing so many issues, like substance abuse, violence, and suicide, she said she still had a sense of hope. Nookmis was at the clinic to encourage individuals and families to reconnect with their Anishinaabe ways. She would speak to them in Anishinaabe, and she even spoke to me in her language when she could not express her thoughts in English. She would ask a community worker to translate what she said so that I understood her teachings. I recall sitting beside her for a quite a while, listening and learning. She even taught me a few Anishinaabe words! Nookmis even encouraged me to continue doing what I was doing. She so appreciated that I travelled from far to help her community. Nookmis exuded warmth and a calming, quiet confidence and her presence was never questioned and always appreciated by all. At the clinic, we were all inspired by this Elder's sense of hope and her wisdom. As a result, we worked closely with the community workers to organize a youth camp where Elders and youth made bannock bread, went hunting in the bush and fishing together, and the youth learned the Anishinaabe ways of living off and respecting the land.

AMBIVALENT RELATIONSHIP WITH THE INDIAN ACT

Indigenous peoples lack trust in government and confidence as many feel that government is not listening to them or really interested in changing the health and socioeconomic conditions. At times, as many First Nation people have expressed to me, it appears that government is apprehensive to relinquish power and authority to encourage community-based programs or initiatives. In Canada, the Department of Aboriginal Affairs and Northern Development in particular remains tied to the Indian Act, which is the legislation that was developed in 1876 and governs all essential programs and services in First Nation communities.[4] This legislation was developed to endorse the colonial agenda. Indigenous scholar, Henderson (2007) notes the disconnect between indigenous histories, laws, and cultures and the imposed system of colonial rule found in the Indian Act. I have noted an ambivalent relationship to the Indian Act with First Nations who on one end, feel that this piece of legislation is archaic and paternalistic, while others feel that the act itself does protect their special Aboriginal status within the Canadian Confederation and their specific rights. While the Indian Act has undergone numerous amendments since 1876, today it largely retains its original form. Consequently, the progress with programs governed by the Indian Act has been incremental and the progress is mostly as a result of communities working together with both federal and provincial/territorial governments. I have actually noticed incremental progress for programs that remain tied to the Act. For instance, two particular social development programs, that is, the Income Assistance program and the Child and Family Services program are showing some progress in terms of moving from a reactive stance to a more proactive approach. Both programs are founded on Western concepts of welfare and the removal of children from their homes. The Income Assistance program is currently implementing skills development training to ensure youth can gain employment in their communities. "Income Assistance benefits for these individuals will depend on participation in the necessary training as per current practice in most provinces" (Government of Canada 2013). I met some First Nation welfare recipients who have difficulty engaging in such active measures to engage back into the workforce because they feel it is their right as stipulated by the Indian Act to obtain their monthly welfare cheques like their parents and grandparents did. I think this sense of entitlement is a natural, direct result of colonialism as the Indian Act clearly aimed to assimilate the First Nations, and many believe to annihilate. Many Income Assistance case workers in First Nation communities have expressed to me that this attitude is a challenge for them to overcome. Another challenge for several First Nation communities is the limited capacity to deliver the enhanced service delivery for this program. There remains a sense of dependence on government programs that is so ingrained some communities feel crippled by the Act, which forced "Indians" to live on reserves and imposed limitations on them so that, in the end, they would choose full assimilation. As much as there is a strong need and desire to provide services to First Nations living on reserves comparable to those being offered to neighboring municipalities within the province or territory, many times the capacity infrastructure is absent. The reserve system was not founded on ensuring First Nations would have the services required to live in a sustainable fashion. The intended consequence of the Indian Act was to culturally oppress and eradicate First Nations and the unintended consequence was that it led to the "Indian problem" or "Aboriginal issues" in Canada, as the First Peoples were not eradicated after all. Many scholars believe that existing health and socio-economic development programs derive from policies that are redemptive and reactive, and only address indigenous suffering (Alfred 2005; Irlbacher-Fox 2009). As Palmater, an indigenous scholar (2014, 28) contends: ". . . the barrier towards real, substantive change in the relationship between indigenous Nations and Canada is the failure by Canada to stop framing Indians as a 'problem' and to abandon their policy objective of eliminating Indians. No agreement, law, or program will ever reverse the legislative extinction trend unless and until Canada accepts that indigenous peoples are not mere memories from a time gone by, but are in fact here to stay."

What I have noticed is that when First Nations draw from their own philosophical and cultural ways in the implementation of such Indian Act–tied programs, that is when progress is visible and sustained as the programs are re-interpreted to reflect the community's priorities and aspirations. The other social development program is the Child and Family Services program, where in the past years there has been a shift toward a more proactive, enhanced prevention approach, which entails working with the children and the families, provide essential supports, and only place the children in care as a last resort. There are currently over twenty-seven thousand Aboriginal children in care outside the parental home; therefore, this enhanced prevention approach that is being effectively implemented in some provinces should help decrease this amount of children currently in care (Government of Canada, July 3, 2013). "Since 2007, the department has been working with willing First Nations, provincial and Yukon Territory partners to transition jurisdictions to an Enhanced Prevention Focused Approach. Today, this approach is being implemented in six provinces reaching about 68 percent of on reserve First Nations children" (Government of Canada, July 3, 2013). Many initiatives funded by the Government of Canada and led by First Nation communities have had significant and meaningful impact, such as the healing initiatives supported by the Aboriginal Healing Foundation, which was funded by the federal government's Gathering Strength: Canada's Aboriginal Action Plan in 1998 and the Indian Residential School Settlement Agreement in 2007. There have also been several policies and legislative tools that have emerged to encourage First Nations to move beyond the confines of the Indian Act, such as First Nation led self-government processes. I will further elaborate on this in chapter 4.

We have also witnessed incrementalism with respect to decisions from the Supreme Court of Canada that has supported First Nation/Inuit/Métis rights, cultures, and languages. Several court decisions have recognized and affirmed Aboriginal rights and title and help clarify the federal government's legal obligations. These decisions have provided indigenous people of Canada the impetus to advance their agenda (Smith and Sterritt 2010). On June 26, 2014, the Supreme Court of Canada granted declaration of Aboriginal title to more than 1,700 square kilometres of land in British Columbia to the Tsilhqot'in First Nation, and this is the first time the court has made such a ruling recognizing Aboriginal title, and the requirement for consent not consultation alone with Aboriginal partners in the pursuit of resource development projects. This ruling is considered a landmark decision and a game changer (Politics 2014; Bains 2014).[5] I will further illustrate in chapter 6 how the Supreme Court of Canada tends to support Aboriginal rights, which forces the government of Canada to rethink its policies to more effectively support reconciliation. Some argue that where the Indian Act reduces Aboriginal identity to a registered status, the Supreme Court of Canada reduces it to practices, customs, and traditions (Neveu 2010). Nonetheless, recent decisions demonstrate how the Supreme Court of Canada continues to protect indigenous interests and that *both* federal and provincial or territorial governments need to work more effectively with their indigenous partners. There also has been a growing number of case law in favor of indigenous peoples influencing many recent out-of-court settlements on issues of lack of government consultation or infringement of Aboriginal rights (Irlbacher-Fox 2009).

In terms of the profound mistrust in government, to me, it makes complete sense and I have always understood and never questioned why indigenous peoples are apprehensive of government, evaluators, and researchers as they are frustrated and discouraged with policies, evaluations, and research that do not lead to meaningful, community-relevant results. Too often enough research is completed for the sake of research rather than for the benefit of the people, the actual subjects of the research. And too often, policies are developed and implemented without their consent and/or input. Nonetheless, as I will illustrate in chapter 4, there are increasing efforts toward participatory research, collaborative approaches, increasing partnerships, and recognition of the effectiveness of community-led initiatives and plans. This progress I believe initiated with indigenous peoples' apprehension, anger, and resistance to paternalistic, Western-dominated research paradigms and policies that are not leading to change, and the nonindigenous researchers are finally listening and realizing that community-centered approaches are most effective. This progress is incremental, and it will hopefully continue to evolve. As researchers, Shepherd and Persad (2011, 28) clearly affirm, "It is up to government to adjust, not First Nations." And I would add that the most critical part of that adjustment is for government and researchers to understand and validate the mistrust and the apprehension in order to build a rapport that could lead to meaningful work. We also need to develop policies and research that support changing oppressive circumstances and accommodate indigeneity rather than require indigenous people to cope with such circumstances and dismiss their indigeneity (Irlbacher-Fox 2009; Alfred and Corntassel 2005).

THE SETTLER IN ME

The underlying element that I have always been upfront with is that I am a settler, that I possess a cultural identity that was not oppressed, and that I can never really know what it feels like to be culturally wounded and traumatized. I never denied my existence or tried to cover it up. I could easily pass as a Cree, Ojibwe, or Mohawk person given my dark complexion and almond-shaped eyes, as I am often asked from which indigenous community I am from. As soon as I say that I am of Italian origin, the indigenous individuals I meet always want to know more about me, my culture, and my language. The reality of who I am and that I am a descendant of the settlers was never left unspoken. Oftentimes both I and my indigenous partners just move beyond this tension as it quickly dissipates and is replaced with mutual respect, and a willingness to get to know each other and learn *from* each other. Yet as part of my responsibility as an ally and advocate, I need to be continually aware of how words and actions can be harmful. I once introduced myself at a think-tank symposium I had organized with government and indigenous scholars and community development experts as a "change agent." A renowned indigenous Elder in the room came to me at the break and said,

> Nadia, I feel that you have good intentions in your heart, so I ask that you be careful in using the term 'agent,' as there are residential school survivors here and elsewhere you may meet in your path who may be triggered emotionally by the term. It can remind them of the 'Indian agents' who had taken them away from their parents to be brought to residential schools. I understood what you meant but be careful.

Another life lesson for me: to remain cautious with my word choice. I so appreciated this Elder's openness to share her insight with me to help me enrich my understanding.

In my career, I have experienced the two polar opposites of trust and mistrust, both inherently powerful and intense. Interestingly, when I became a public servant, the acceptance was not as immediate as when I was a clinician. Many felt I was now employed by the government who caused the issues facing Aboriginal peoples today and so why should they even bother trusting me. I was asked once to be a keynote speaker at a First Nation conference on supporting sustainable communities. I was asked to talk about how we in my department are working together with First Nations to make a difference in communities. There were five hundred First Nation community members, social workers, and nurses in the conference hall. I was introduced, and the first slide of my presentation appeared on the large screen, with "Indian and Northern Affairs Canada Working with First Nations—Moving towards Sustainable Communities."[6] I was excited to share my first ever experience in government, and that is that a policy framework was developed in collaboration with First Nation social service providers. Soon after the title slide of my presentation appeared, silence blanketed the room, and all I can hear are my footsteps as I walked toward the podium. I wondered why it got so quiet. Suddenly a woman in the audience says, "Why should I trust this white bureaucrat! This is complete bullshit!" I heard her loud and clear. My knees started knocking, my hands shaking, and my palms sweating. I focused on my breathing and tried to stay calm. I came face to face with the profound mistrust and anger First Nations have toward this federal department in particular and rightly so. I kept thinking that maybe if I tell them I worked in communities for sixteen years as a therapist they may listen, they may take me seriously, they may trust me. I realized that that was not good enough. I recall lowering my head, closing my eyes for ten seconds, and asking my deceased grandparents to give me the strength I needed to be honest and upfront with this individual in particular and the audience overall. I placed my speaking points aside and said, "You are right. You shouldn't trust me—at least not yet. I can't and can never know how you feel or truly understand what cultural oppression is or feels like. What I'd like you to know is I am willing to learn from you. I am willing to listen, and I really am willing to work with you." I scanned the crowd and noticed people nodding and smiling in appreciation of my honesty. I too felt relieved from not expressing any unnecessary and empty jargon but moreover, from expressing truthfully. I was pleased I once again followed my gut. The presentation was well received after that tension was recognized and validated. That woman, who initially yelled out, later came to one of my workshops and thanked me for being real. This experience changed not only my presentation that day, but it transformed me in becoming a better person and advocate. It was an experience where I was openly judged and criticized in front of a large crowd and my vulnerability and fear were in the foreground. I acknowledged my fears as well as the mistrust that was most likely in many of the individuals in the room and not in that one woman alone.

I have always felt that it is my responsibility as a Canadian to recognize the colonial injustices and the effects still being felt today, and to appreciate the collective efforts of cultural revitalization. For the longest time, governments and the Western society as a whole invalidated indigenous knowledge and intelligence where the Western counterpart was considered superior and what should be adopted in order to integrate into society and be prosperous.

As a result, there was a significant loss of cultural ways, loss of parenting skills, and a loss of community connectedness. Thus, it is only natural in my mind that the mistrust and anger toward the government especially remain quite profound. I realized early on that I needed to listen attentively and with compassion to understand the complexities of the mistrust and anger, and most importantly, validate the individual's feelings. Listening to the perpetrator as described earlier (Maddy's father) was such a challenge for me, but again in that discomfort, I came face-to-face with the effects of colonialism not just on one individual but also others, and it was an invaluable learning experience. I have often said to indigenous individuals, and still do today, "It is okay to not trust me. I can never truly understand and experience the feelings you have, but I can listen to you, and learn from you." Most often as soon as I validate the mistrust, the tension begins to dissipate, the encounter transforms to a rapport, leading to an engagement and exchange, and a profound sense of appreciation is experienced.

At another First Nation-led and -organized annual conference, I presented on a project I was working on, which related to the quality of life in remote communities. The project focused on six remote communities where they defined what life is like in communities that are isolated—some were fly-in communities with no roads connecting them to other communities. Quality of life was defined as a combination of strengths, like a stronger cultural identity and sense of community, as well as challenges, such as, high transportation costs and being isolated from emergency medical services, to name a few. When I presented the results of this study at this conference, I had two individuals in the room who were extremely resistant and it was visible from the start of my presentation. They eventually voiced their concern that "how can someone from Ottawa know anything about living in a remote community?" I validated their concern and explained that my only intention was to share the results of the study in hopes to raise awareness as remote communities rarely get the attention they require, especially within the policy circles. They nodded, but I felt that this was still insufficient to appease their concerns and to help deconstruct their resistance. They then stood up and said, "We challenge you to actually come visit a remote community and really see with your own eyes what life is like. We'd like to take you there." Two months later, after trying to gather some extra funds, convince senior management that this was a great idea, and gather support for my efforts to develop more relevant policies for remote communities, I visited two remote communities with my conference participants and an Elder from the region. I was greeted with warmth as I listened to presentations by community members that spoke to their frustrations with the lack of federal funding, the lack of services, and broken promises. They were promised a heater in the gymnasium of the school, and they were promised broadband Internet so that they would not have to ship in books for the children, which was so extremely expensive given that they have to pay the transport of the books by weight. Everything is transported to the community via a motorboat. In the end, the communities were so appreciative that I showed interest and that I promised I would bring what I heard back to my colleagues in government. While on the floater plane, on our return, the two conference participants expressed their appreciation of my following through with their "dare." The Elder said, "We thank you for being compassionate and real."

When I returned to my office, as I had promised the community representatives, I continued to engage in teleconference meetings with the regional colleagues and other fellow colleagues at headquarters. We contacted the First Nation technology expert in the region, and together, we worked on analyzing the situation, discovering the missing links, and networking further with partners who can support the installation of a functional Internet broadband that would benefit this particular remote community. This experience can simply be defined by "silo-busting" and ensuring we all work together to be most effective on the front line. A few months after my visit, the installation was complete, and the community members had access to the Internet. A meaningful result of this trip was that we all remained in contact with each other. The youth in the community school were so happy and proud that they produced a video to show their appreciation. They can now use school books online rather than pay expensive transportation costs (flight and then boat fees) to get the books to the community. They can also access the Indspire Institute online tools and resources for indigenous students, educators, parents, and community members. These online tools are helping to increase high school completion rates among youth. It provides an online community network to find classroom resources and links to community-based projects (Indspire 2014).

RESONANCE AND RELEVANCE

When therapy, initiatives, projects, or policies make sense and have meaningful impact on the ground, the repercussions of resonance help propel a community into healing, rebuilding, and redeveloping, and change is sustained. I recall organizing group art-therapy sessions with youth and Elders together in the bushcamp and the setting was a wigwam or teepee. I asked an Elder to share their life narrative with the youth, who would in turn draw about what they heard and then show the drawing to the Elder. This experience exemplified the power of resonance and how it evokes sameness and enables appreciation (Wikan 2012), where the Elders felt empowered to share their stories, felt listened to and acknowledged by their youth, and where the youth felt empowered from listening and learning from their Elders, and then, translating what they heard through their own artistic self-expression. Both the Elders and youth connected themselves with familiar people, with places, and with the past, which provides feelings of ownership of history, a sense of shared meaning and cultural identity. The resonance experienced by both the Elders and the youth nurtured their sense of belongingness and for many of them, it either ignited or contributed to their healing process and reconnection to their cultural pride. Each individual was given a voice, and the artwork created was also symbolic of their voice and the experience. This exchange opened up possibilities for self-transformation. For me, this experience was one of the highlights of my career. I too experienced resonance. Resonance demands an effort at feeling-thought as it entails attending to the concerns and intentions from which expressions emanate (Wikan 2012). Here, my experience was one where I tried to grasp and appreciate the meanings of what was being shared and interpreted that did not reside in words, and create my personal meaning from "the meeting of one experiencing subject with another" (57), and the sharing of personal narratives. I appreciated as well as experienced the relevance of the people's lived predicaments. Resonance entails implicating oneself actively and emotionally in the other's world rather than being a marginal observer. As Wikan (2012, 77) clearly states, "where culture separates, resonance bridges," and a shared space is created. The shared space was for the Elders, youth, and me beyond bridging the affective and cognitive levels of experience—it was a shared space that resonated with each of our spirits. The resonance I experienced was an embodied response where sensual experiences and emotional responses contributed to this memorable encounter. The scent of the fresh pine needles in the wigwam, the old storied canvas walls, with some sections that were hand-stitched, the crackling ashes in the center fire smoking lightly, and the warmth I felt, like it was my second home.

Listening

What resonates for me is Anishinaabe social worker Cheryle Partridge's (2010, 40) definition of listening as "using every fibre of my being, not only my ears." Listening is fundamental in the therapeutic setting, and it is as fundamental in my current work with my indigenous partners. As a Haida Elder shared with me, listening keeps tradition alive, and what is said remains sacred because it contributes to one's learning process, if what is said is heard and if what is said evokes meaning. Listening is a discursive practice that helps connect people to place, and as I learned from Elders, listening allows one to actively coexist and coparticipate in a largely nonverbal, spiritual world (cf. Carbaugh 1999). I cannot stress enough the importance of listening and how people, especially settlers, have to learn to listen more acutely. What I have noticed among many nonindigenous people is that listening attentively, reflectively, and with humility remains a challenge (Regan 2010). In order for us all, indigenous and nonindigenous, to engage in rethinking, restorying, and decolonizing, we need to engage in effective dialogue, which is founded on effective listening.

In Marcia Krawll's (1994) enlightening work on *Understanding the Role of Healing in Aboriginal Communities*, she describes the role of government in the healing and development of communities and outlines a protocol that governments should respect especially in relation to community development. The protocol is based on understanding, respect, advocacy, partnership, and support rather than imposition. Krawll's research is supported by rich ethnographic material from interviews with Aboriginal people, and a common plea for many was for governments to understand Aboriginal people better and how this understanding is at the basis of more effective working relationships. According to the participants, this understanding begins with listening more attentively and observing firsthand in communities to understand their life experiences. "Listening involves clarifying what is read or heard and not simply referring back to what is familiar or believed to be known. The opportunity to work towards partnership will be reflected in the willingness to compare and review any differences in terminology or concepts which may differ from one's own" (Krawll 1994, 72). In addition to listening and observing firsthand, the participants highlighted the need to create an open, direct, and consistent dialogue between the government and communities. One participant said: "I would like to see the government get more involved in the 'circle' approach where people can speak equally and be heard equally" (Krawll 1994, 73). I applied this protocol as a clinician, and I continue to apply it in my work as an advocate. As I have illustrated, listening alone is not sufficient in developing a dialogic exchange based on trust. Empathic listening is critical. Listening with every fiber of my being naturally entails being empathic. Listening and empathy for me are interdependent, and can be transformative because our whole being is involved (Regan 2010, 191–192).

Listening and Empathy

Engaging in empathic awareness and gaining insight into the other's life world entails imaginatively reconstructing their experience as well as creating a safe place where they can express their innermost thoughts and emotions. The prerequisites to feeling safe include openness, respect, and attentiveness, which lead to exploring new ways of being. As I listen to my patients, partners, or colleagues, I also have a strong willingness to learn from them. Together we cultivate a shared horizon of understanding, and the experience of empathy does not only entail understanding another but also the experience of being understood (Throop 2010). The empathy experienced is similar to what Hollan (2012) describes as "complex empathy." "From an ethnographic perspective, [. . .] complex empathy is never 'neutral,' but rather is always found embedded in a moral context, which affects both its likelihood and means of expression, and its social, emotional, and even its political and economic, consequences" (Hollan 2012, 72). Complex empathy requires time and intent and not necessarily a sense of selflessness but a strong sense of self, ready to take the time to listen and understand the experience of another.

Listening and empathy go hand in hand and so are not viewed as distinct processes within several indigenous cosmologies I have experienced and learned from. Empathy entails listening and understanding another's experience of resonance. Both empathy and listening are a type of metacommunication. Like empathy, listening involves the affective, cognitive, and spiritual realms and is not necessarily linked to hearing words from another through verbal discourse. Importance is placed on what is not said, such as, on body language, as is on what is said. Situating oneself in listening, in dialogue, and in being with others is critical as it nurtures self-awareness. Listening and empathy help establish trust, build relationships and promote intersubjectivity. Intersubjectivity is a fundamental dimension of human experience, and it can lead to mutual understanding as it is a condition for the possibility of communication and human interaction (Duranti 2010). I believe it is our responsibility as human beings to try to engage in the complexities of empathy, to show respect for others as well as ourselves, to acknowledge one another's being in the world and to learn from intersubjective existential realities. "[T]he vicissitudes of empathy can disclose as much about the possibilities and limits of self-understanding as it can about capacities to connect with and understand others" (Throop 2010, 780). My work as a clinician, anthropologist, and advocate revealed aspects of my own being that were previously concealed to me, and I discovered these through my intersubjective encounters. Some of the aspects of my being that I discovered include my quiet confidence and sense of calm in crisis situations. These self-discoveries became tools that I enhanced and strengthened the more I interacted and the more I was faced with unsettling situations. My sense of self became a resource in interaction and/or dialogue that was at times harmonious and at other times, disharmonious and more challenging. As noted by Sones (2010, 2), "self-awareness is an experiential and values-based learning process, with the most change accomplished through relationship." We constitute our sense of selves in interaction and dialogue with others. In my intersubjective encounters, I tend to place emphasis on the interdynamics of the discourse, which include the lived predicaments we each bring to the interaction, the lived experience we create as a result of the interaction as well as self-reflection.

As anthropologists and public servants, we need to refine our ways of listening and attending to better understand people's concerns, which will lead to rebuilding relationships and building a sense of interconnectedness. A critical first step in the rebuilding is the acknowledgment of the wrongdoing that was done onto indigenous peoples, which as Govier (2003, 84), a Canadian philosopher, contends, helps communicate a recognition of human dignity. The experience of being understood often fosters not only a sense of safety but also a reconnection to a sense of belongingness, and I have witnessed this both in the clinical setting and in my current encounters with others as well as within myself but only through ongoing dialogue, empathetic listening, and mutual respect. The sense of belongingness intensifies and grows once an individual connects with his/her cultural identity. Chandler and Lalonde (1998) show how cultural continuity contributes to a decrease in suicide among First Nations in Canada, and so, when an individual connects with his/her cultural identity, the individual then reconnects with his/her cultural pride and personal sense of belongingness. The increased suicide rates among many First Nations, Inuit, and Métis communities is most often related to cultural shame, despair, and a detached sense of place-based existence (Alfred and Corntassel 2005).[7] From dialogic exchange we create dialogic networks that are founded on trust, respect, an openness to learn from each other, leading to deriving a sense of place from the partnership, which are instrumental to effecting change and promoting healing and community development. As I write this, I have discovered that when I am faced with the mistrust and resistance, it is not my skills in relationship building alone but more so my transparency and authenticity that are paramount in deconstructing the mistrust and rebuilding the trust. I am transparent and authentic in that I do not deny the settler in me. I want to learn from the past so that we do not repeat the same mistakes, and I do not contribute to intergenerational colonialism. I too need to heal from our collective history and transform my guilt and shame into action, concrete tangibles that have meaningful impact on the front line in First Nation, Inuit, and Métis communities.

I adamantly refuse to be neutral or complacent about Canada's colonial legacy. Knowing all the injustices that indigenous people have experienced, I cannot fathom being neutral. Neutrality definitely is "an expression of settler symbolic violence, or power over, indigenous people" (Regan 2010, 39). Too often, I have noticed people listening but with a judgmental stance or in disbelief, which in my opinion exemplify disembodied empathy and disengagement. We cannot be neutral about cultural genocide, nor can we rationalize it. Neutrality reflects an individual's choice to not really engage, listen, and share elements of his/her life story or cultural identity. As a Métis Elder recently advised me, along with a nonindigenous group of front line community workers, "if sharing is not reciprocated then the interaction is not meaningful." For me, neutrality equates with willful ignorance (Schaefli and Godlewska 2014), which is a colonial strategy. Willful ignorance or strategic unknowing is sanctioned and taught through our educational system, and it

remains a significant barrier to reconciliation. The ignorance of nonindigenous people I often encounter is founded on the belief that the present crises
in some indigenous communities are not related to the injustices they have
experienced. Many prefer to ignore the unpleasant facts of our national history, and I agree with Govier (2003, 86) that if the events and harms toward
indigenous peoples are denied or ignored, then "we will be unable to stand in
an honest and constructive relationship with them." I believe that such ignorance and denial promote intergenerational trauma and colonialism, and because ignorance justifies exclusion, it continues to pose a substantial barrier
to reconciliation (Schaefli and Godlewska 2014), which I will further elaborate in chapter 6. Ultimately, we each have a choice to be actively engaged
in reconciliation, to be aware of our colonial history and indigenous cultural
resilience or to remain ignorant, complacent, and do nothing. The latter is in
and of itself a moral failure (Martin 2014; Barker 2010), but it does remain
an individual's choice, and I believe it is a risk to be unsettled by our past and
become engaged, yet it is riskier to do nothing and remain colonial and
ignorant.

Settler-allies are those who are capable of listening (Alfred and Corntassel 2005) and who listen with an open mind and spirit. Reconciliation entails
an intercultural dialogue, a process not an end goal that is founded on mutual
respect, responsibility, openness, sharing, and recognition (Neveu 2010).
Nonindigenous scholars, activists, clinicians, and bureaucrats need to establish relationships with indigenous peoples rather than engage in detached
discourses about them (Turner 2006; Neveu 2010). I enter relationships with
my indigenous partners with my ethical principles, my personal moral obligation, and commitment, and I can say that every encounter begins with open
dialogue and mutual respect. I do not present myself as the expert, the therapist, the anthropologist, the bureaucrat, or the activist. I present myself as an
individual with a willingness and readiness to help balance the impact of
crises that led to weaknesses, with the existing assets and strengths, and to
encourage culturally based healing driven by the individual and the community. In my encounters, if the mistrust is present, it is acknowledged and often
dissipates as a result of the validation, and a relationship is formed. Some are
temporary, while others are long-lasting alliances.

NOTES

1. This is often referred to as an animal-doctor relationship among the Crees, which I
explore in Ferrara (2004).
2. Currently, as Blackstock (2003, 2010) contends, the proportion of First Nation children
in child welfare has reached record levels eclipsing both the "sixties scoop" and residential
schools. In February 2007, the First Nations Child and Family Caring Society and the Assembly of First Nations filed a complaint alleging that the Government of Canada's provision of
First Nation child and family services was inequitable and discriminatory under the Canadian

Human Rights Act. The Canadian Human Rights Tribunal on First Nation child welfare with over six thousand witnesses has become the most watched court case on children's rights in Canadian history.

3. Vicarious trauma is also referred to as compassion fatigue or secondary trauma, where listening to and witnessing the suffering and pain of others overcomes the therapist or helping professional's coping skills (Jordan 2010).

4. Under the Indian Act, First Nation communities are defined as reserves and the Act authorizes the Canadian federal government to regulate and administer the affairs and day-to-day lives of registered "Indians" and reserve communities. The Act was designed to assimilate First Nation peoples into Canadian society. This authority has ranged from overarching political control, such as imposing governing structures on Aboriginal communities in the form of band councils, to control over the rights of "Indians" to practice their culture and traditions. The Act has also enabled the government to determine the land base of these groups in the form of reserves, and to define who qualifies as "Indian" in the form of "Indian status" (Government of Canada, December 9, 2013).

5. This Supreme Court of Canada decision, indexed as *Tsilhqot'in Nation v. British Columbia*, is also referred to as the Roger William's decision as he is the former chief of the Tsilhqot'in First Nation who had filed a claim seeking recognition of Aboriginal title to two tracts of land in the Tsilhqot'in traditional territory (*Tsilhqot'in Nation v. British Columbia* 2014). In 2012, a British Columbia Court of Appeal ruling gave the Tsilhqot'in sweeping rights to hunt, trap and trade in its traditional territory. However, the Court of Appeal agreed with the federal and provincial governments that the Tsilhqot'in must identify specific sites where its people once lived, rather than assert a claim over a broad area. First Nations across Canada denounced this judgment as a discriminatory ruling that denigrates and disregards Aboriginal ways of life, and in particular their distinctive systems of law and land use. Consequently, the Tsilhqot'in Nation brought its appeal before the Supreme Court of Canada on November 7, 2013. The Tsilhqot'in called on the Court to continue on the path that it has charted, to end the long era of denial and discrimination, and to provide long-overdue recognition of Aboriginal title on the ground, as the starting point for true and lasting reconciliation. On June 26, 2014, the Supreme Court of Canada's decision did just that according to many First Nations (Politics 2014), and it has created a higher standard of engagement with Aboriginal people who have been granted title. This ruling is expected to have significant implications for future natural resource development in British Columbia and across the country in areas that impact on Aboriginal communities. It will also have impacts on treaty negotiations where First Nations may choose to seek support through the courts rather than at treaty tables (Bains 2014).

6. The federal department I work in was formerly called "Indian and Northern Affairs Canada." It is now referred to as "Aboriginal Affairs and Northern Development Canada."

7. Holder and Corntassel (2002, 149) also assert that an individual's psychic health is contingent on group affiliation in the context of indigenous rights discourse and how collective and individual rights are interdependent.

Chapter Four

Translating Lived Realities

Many still have difficulty in recognizing the cultural diversity among First Nation, Inuit, and Métis peoples. Moreover, there is a wide spectrum from communities in a crisis and vulnerable state to those that are high functioning and sustainable. A related challenge is to apply a differentiated approach to policy development with respect to the communities and their distinct realities. We have much to learn from the communities themselves, and we need to develop policies that reflect community priorities. There are many community-led initiatives in First Nation communities that are successful and meaningful at the community level. Place-based approach to policy development is all about enabling the capacity and providing the tools for such community-driven initiatives to take place. Place-based approach can be defined as evidence-based policy making. There are many communities who are thriving and have been enabling other communities to learn from their experiences. What is unfortunate is that other Canadians and North Americans overall, rarely hear about communities who have been successful and have become self-sustaining.

My objective in sharing, translating lived experiences of both my patients and informants, is to enlighten, educate, appreciate differences, unique life experiences, and evoke sameness and a sense of connectedness. As an art therapist, I translated interpretations of artwork and art-making, emotional expressions of my patients in order to build credibility of the profession, share the successes I witnessed, but most importantly, share the personal narratives. I hope to remain faithful to the narratives I have heard, which I consider to be rich and many reflective of indigenous knowledge, which is equally important if not more than academic theories or knowledge. In translating lived realities shared with me, I do not claim my translation as the final or only interpretation as there is much that has eluded my gaze, listening, and translation (cf. Kelm 1998). And I am fully aware that my interpretations depend on how I, as an anthropologist, am historically, culturally, politically, and morally positioned (Narayan 1993). The translation I am referring to is the interpretation of a narrative, an account that speaks to an individual's life experience, as well as the shared space we experienced and created together as a result of the individual sharing the narrative and me listening and validating it.

TRANSLATING HEALING

I would like to highlight the translation process of personal growth that occurs in the later stages of therapy. The translation from therapy into the individual's "outside world" is critical in order to ensure that their healing process continues once therapy ends. In my experience as an art therapist with indigenous patients, the therapy was not viewed as a separate activity as among my nonindigenous patients; it became part of their everyday life. When termination of the therapy was introduced with my indigenous patients, I was faced with great bewilderment and resistance as they could not understand why something good had to end. For instance, with Luke, ending art therapy with me was quite the challenge, especially after two and a half years of weekly, individual sessions and this included transitioning him back to his home community with his family. In his last session, he drew a picture of him sleeping under a tree and he was dreaming of his art therapy experience with me (symbolized by a heart) and that when he was going to wake up it will just be a memory. There was a desire to create transitional linkages, like a drawing journal, to help transfer their healing and self-reflection from the art-therapy experience into their everyday life. Similarly, Tom, a thirty-eight-year-old Cree bushman I saw for two years in therapy, who became a self-discovered artist through his art therapy experience, created a journal as a transitional tool.[1] Tom grew attached to this tool as it symbolized his self-discovery, his art-therapy experience, and his re-integration back into his home community. He had expressed that the drawing journal replaced his need to turn to alcohol as an escape. The journal had such meaning for him as he would draw his dreams, fears, his grief about his parents' death, and his accomplishments as a bushman and hunter. For Luke and Tom as well as other indigenous patients I worked with, the translation was interpreted as an interconnection between the therapeutic experience and life outside therapy, and value was placed on nurturing the memory of the healing, and the journal symbolized this in a tangible way. The therapy my indigenous patients experienced also played a part in their decolonization experience as it enabled their reconnection to their sense of belongingness.

DECOLONIZING THE POLICY WORLD

"When the 'facts' relevant to policy-making are seen as constituted by the particular contexts and experiences, rather than as external objective truths, governments cannot generate meaningful policy knowledge on their own, detached from the problems at hand or distant from the people living with them" (Bradford 2005, 6). The translation of lived realities in policy development occurs at the intersection between research and community experiential knowledge, where research is deconstructed and community knowledge is integrated, and where policy is defined by experience-near knowledge and relevant cultural values and not by "external objective truths" that lack meaning on the front line. For effective and meaningful policy development, researchers and public servants need to listen to people and map their interactions in their communities, their places, and understand and appreciate their assets (Bradford 2005). The emphasis is on endogenous, dynamic assets rather than on the role of exogenous investments that view communities as homogenous. Place-based approach to policy development emphasizes bottom-up, locally designed and owned strategies aimed at promoting potential in local communities. Examples of place-based initiatives in indigenous communities in Canada include comprehensive community planning,[2] strategic planning, land use planning, integrated area planning, and self-government agreements. Such community-driven and community-paced projects tend to derive from an inclusive and participatory process that empowers local people to engage in action planning based on local capacity, knowledge, skills, and aspirations.

The place, the community, the home has significant meaning, and for many indigenous peoples, place is intimately linked to one's cultural identity. Indigenous community planning requires that it be done in the community with the people of that place, inclusive of experiential knowledge, and it requires a commitment to political, social, economic, and environmental change (Walker, Jojola, and Natcher 2013). Place-based approach to policy development supports the decolonization process. By encouraging community members to translate policies on the ground, to re-interpret policies to include locally meaningful realities—once implemented, the policies will lead to better outcomes, in turn, leading to sustained progress—progress that is owned by the community. This sense of ownership is critical in the experience of decolonization, as well as the recognition that "indigenous planning has always existed. Indigenous communities predate colonialism and were planned according to their own traditions and sets of practices" (Walker, Jojola, and Natcher 2013, 5).

When I first started working in government, I was given the lead on a project to develop a social development policy framework. We worked in collaboration with a national Aboriginal organization, representatives from the federal regional offices, provinces and territories, and most importantly, First Nation social service providers. There was significant apprehension and mistrust from First Nation representatives toward the government workers, especially during the initial phase. Every time we would meet, the apprehension was expressed as well as their anger with respect to the third world-type socioeconomic conditions First Nations Elders, families, and children are experiencing in communities. Many of my government colleagues were uncomfortable with this whole process as they just wanted to get the work done and push it through the system. It was a long and arduous process, but in the end, a policy framework was developed, and it embedded First Nation cultural values in the vision statements for each program as well as the principles. The First Nation social service practitioners clearly shaped this policy framework, and they often voiced that these policies affect those on the front line and not those in the government offices. They aspired that this policy framework would be unlike most government policies, which are devoid of locally meaningful realities.

My contribution as an anthropologist in the development of the policy framework described above was to focus on the interconnections made among the networks involved, that is, the First Nation partners, the federal, provincial, and nongovernment organizations, and explore the interactions between public policy and community interests. As Wedel, Shore, Feldman, and Lathrop (2005) claim, we cannot treat policy without reference to the sociocultural contexts in which it is embedded, and so, there is value added to an anthropological approach to the study of policy, as it "incorporates the full realm of processes and relations involved in the production of policy: from the policy makers and their strategic initiatives to the locals who invariably shape and mediate policy while translating and implementing it into action" (Wedel et al. 2005, 34). Anthropology is ideally suited to explore the underpinnings of policy because policies are cultural, social, and political phenomena (Feldman and Wedel 2004). Anthropology of public policy forces anthropologists to rethink "the field" as a site of ethnography, where the focus is on the process of "studying through" the source of the policy through those affected on the front line by the policy. As Wedel and Feldman (2005, 2) articulate, "'studying through' can illuminate how different organizational and everyday worlds are interconnected across time and space." Given that policy-making and implementation is hardly a linear process leading to predetermined outcomes, it becomes critical to analyze the complexity and ambiguity of this process and how policy outcomes may contradict the original intention of the policy-maker, yet the outcomes are a result of a reinterpretation by those on the ground (Wedel and Feldman 2005).[3] Wedel et al. (2005) also note, which I believe rings true, that what happens in the boardroom in terms of policy development has direct repercussions on the front line. I have experienced both extremes of policy development, where on one hand, many still practice the positivist paradigm with top-down process-es dictating the development of policies, like many programs governed by the Indian Act, and on the other hand, as described above, where voices from the grassroots perspective inform the policy development process. By vali-dating all partners or networks involved, I am actively engaged in decoloniz-ing the policy world.

RECOGNIZING AND INTEGRATING SITUATED KNOWLEDGES

Donna Haraway (1988) presents an interesting critique of Western "cultural narratives about objectivity" and she claims that we are actively perceiving, building on translations and specific ways of seeing, that is, ways of life (583). She refers to "situated knowledges," which speaks to the interrelation-ships present within the multistranded microcosm of a community. Situated knowledges nurture connections and unexpected openings in the interpretive process. "Situated knowledges are about communities, not about isolated individuals. The only way to find a larger vision is to be somewhere in the particular" (590). I believe recognizing situated knowledges is highly rele-vant in understanding how policies are translated on the ground, in commu-nities. For instance, we in government support isolated programs, such as economic development, social development programs, diabetes prevention, and suicide prevention to name a few. On the ground, these programs tend to be interpreted and delivered in a more integrated fashion. I had met many individuals who were on welfare and experiencing physical ailments as well as suicidal ideation, and the most effective plan to support these individuals was to focus on ensuring their emotional, physical, and spiritual well-being was being treated while introducing measures to engage them into the work-force. We in government need to focus on the interrelationships among the social determinants of well-being within the community,[4] which include so-cial status, employment, education, social support, and culture. "The social determinants of health are based on universal processes but they take unique form in each society based on its cultural history, politics and economy" (Kirmayer 2012, 150). Rather than focusing on one element at a time or isolating one influential factor from another, recognizing and understanding the social determinants of well-being as well as the situated knowledges within communities would help us better grasp this holistic view and in the end, develop policies that are not only more relevant but also more respon-sive and effective.

I will elaborate further by illustrating efforts related to another file I worked on related to sustainable development and how the department can work toward more effectively supporting the socioeconomic well-being of Aboriginal communities. I was often told by my indigenous partners that everything in communities is related to sustainable development, so it should not be considered a distinct file, separate from other policies and programs. At the federal level, sustainable development has been viewed as a distinct file and so individual efforts by departments created a piecemeal approach. Sustainable development has been viewed as an add-on to existing governmental practices when it should be integral to how business is conducted. In order to effect change and sustain progress, the most recent legislation on sustainable development tasked the federal government with a more coordinated approach amongst its departments, and it noted that the objectives will best be achieved by partnering with indigenous people. The explicit relationship between indigenous people and the natural world and their inherent respect for and need to live in harmony with the natural world equates well with the federal priority area of protecting nature. The long-term presence of indigenous people in their home territories resulted in an understanding of the interactions within their areas gained over time that has evolved into a science called Traditional Ecological Knowledge (TEK), which embodies the notion of a situated knowledge as described above. TEK can be defined as "a cumulative body of knowledge, practice, and belief, evolving by adaptive processes and handed down through generations by cultural transmission, about the relationship of living beings (including humans) with one another and with their environment" (Berkes, Colding, and Folk 2000, 1252). It is a complex founded on knowledge-practice-belief. For the Fourth International Polar Year, traditional knowledge and science merged to gain insights on climate change and adaptation. It is important to recognize how there are two different, yet complementary knowledge systems available to help understand how climate variability and change affect the environment and the people (Barber and Barber 2009, 6). The government is realizing that Traditional Ecological Knowledge can help Canada better understand the impacts of climate change. [5]

It was in this spirit that I had led regionally based Aboriginal Engagement Sessions held around the country to seek input that can be incorporated into the development of the department's sustainable development strategy. These focus groups represented the largest effort to date to seek input from Aboriginal people into the departmental sustainable development strategy. I worked closely with my regional colleagues and Aboriginal community members, maintaining continuity with the previous file and sustaining the relationships I had built since I started working in government. The focus groups expressed that the programming link of the federal strategy is the direct connection for the department to communities. Other recommendations include a desire to see a stronger connection between the department and community understanding of sustainable development. A main point in that connection is about making a more direct link between sustainable development and cultural identity. Overall, the commitments were crafted to be more relevant to the communities. Participants in all focus groups repeatedly asked about ongoing involvement in the development, implementation, and monitoring of the strategy. Participants agreed to become part of regional and national reference groups that stay connected electronically (email, chat room, video/web conferencing, etc.). They expressed the need to instill a sense of ownership in the vision and guiding principles of the national strategy. It was also recommended that the department work with Aboriginal people to formalize the recognition of success stories in sustainable development that will help First Nations, Inuit, Métis, and Northerners learn from each others' successes. As one partner noted, "There may not be a better key to building positive social, political, cultural, and economic prosperity than seeing that others have already been down that path." A national recognition program can serve as an important source of knowledge and inspiration and will benefit Aboriginal people by giving them access to innovative ideas and effective governing approaches related to sustainable development. As a result, the department developed an electronic newsletter that highlights past and current best practices and success stories. Although more can be done in this area of recognition, this is an important initiative yet limited to departmental employees. It needs to be more widespread and accessible to Canadians and North Americans. This is definitely a missing element in our education process and everyone, Aboriginal and non-Aboriginal people, is missing out in not being exposed to such a source of knowledge.

During the Aboriginal Engagement Strategy focus groups, a community councillor was in attendance, and she expressed her concern with respect to communities like her own, which was trying to rebuild as it had been crisis. She said that many community members were engaged in the healing process, but she felt as a leader in the community that more can be done especially to help sustain the community's development. She asked the fellow participants for ideas on how best to support sustainable development. This participant heard about the community planning initiatives that were taking place in the provinces of British Columbia and Saskatchewan. After a fruitful discussion, participants concluded that in order to promote sustainable development, the government needs to support community-driven processes. It led to a recommendation to recognize success stories in sustainable development, as well as to more effectively support First Nation–to–First Nation mentoring. After the focus group session, in my role as knowledge broker,[6] I connected the councillor with a First Nation community in British Columbia to obtain more info on comprehensive community planning.[7] I also connected her with the regional representative in her region, who was able to look into funding to help support the planning process. The community came together, with the commitment of formal and informal leaders and after a few years developed their very own comprehensive community plan, which they named *Giiwedaa* (Ojibwe for "coming home").[8] The community developed a community plan, with a vision, objectives, and identified actions. They decided on their top priorities, which included a housing policy, education strategy, and a land-use plan. The plan is long term and will be monitored on a regular basis.

While working on the sustainable development file, I received a proposal from the Jane Goodall Institute requesting for funds to initiate the Roots and Shoots for Aboriginal Youth Program. The Jane Goodall Institute's Roots and Shoots Program is a global environmental and humanitarian youth program spread over 126 countries around the world. The Roots and Shoots program inspires youth to research, plan, and implement community-based service learning projects. At the time I received the request, my senior management and myself thought that supporting such an initiative and giving it a kick start in Aboriginal communities was well aligned with our departmental sustainable development strategy. Similar to the United States Roots and Shoots Program for Indigenous Youth, the Canadian Roots and Shoots for Aboriginal Youth Program aims to provide teachers and youth in First Nations, Inuit, and Métis communities with the necessary resources and support to engage in youth-led projects that incorporate science and traditional knowledge and teachings to address environmental issues (Jane Goodall Institute Canada 2013). The youth tap into the Traditional Ecological Knowledge that has been passed down for generations, and they experience firsthand how such knowledge allows them to adapt, survive, and thrive within their ecological systems. Several youth-led projects, like community gardens, community outreach activities, and an exchange program were supported through the Roots and Shoots for Aboriginal Youth Program. One particular project was an exchange program where youth in one First Nation community created solar lanterns and sent these to another Roots and Shoots youth program in Haiti. Another project that garnered attention was the Wisdom Keepers Storytellers Narrative, which is a showcase of videos of inspiring and challenging stories from Aboriginal youth across Canada—stories of culture, resilience, spirituality and the environment.[9] They are documentary-style videos that connect their community and culture to issues around people, animals, and the environment. This project integrated grassroots dimensions by applying the guidance and teachings from Elders, and knowledge from oral traditions. An additional project was the Champions of Youth meetings, which helped establish a strong network of champions active in youth engagement, advocates of the Roots and Shoots program. All the Roots and Shoots projects around the world are based on the knowledge-compassion-action-reflection model of learning, listening, empathizing, teaching, and advocating.

There are currently fifty groups of Roots and Shoots Aboriginal youth in action with representation from every province and territory in Canada. Its American counterpart—the United States Roots and Shoots Program for Indigenous Youth—has been around for nearly a decade in the Pine Ridge Indian Reservation in South Dakota. Pine Ridge Indian Reservation is the poorest Native American reservation in the United States with a youth suicide rate four times the national average. On the reservation, the Roots and Shoots youth members' projects have ranged from planting community gardens to establishing farmers markets, initiating water conservation efforts, and so much more. These projects have directly impacted over 4,500 of the 15,521 people living on the Reservation. Roots and Shoots has brought hope to the reservation and empowered young people to become involved in improving their community for people, animals, and the environment (The Jane Goodall Institute 2011; 2013). For some reason, the Roots and Shoots for Aboriginal Youth Program has spread more quickly in Canada than in the United States, and for that reason, Dr. Jane Goodall herself requested to meet with me. She asked me for some support in information sharing and networking with the United States Roots and Shoots program for Native American youth in hopes that it too would gain such needed momentum to spread into other Native American reservations. I contacted my colleagues in the Bureau of Indian Affairs in the United States, and some American academic colleagues specializing in sustainable community development established a working group to help better support the Roots and Shoots Youth Program in particular. I organized monthly teleconference calls where the profile of the Roots and Shoots Program was raised and consequently options for further funding were proposed. This was so successful that Dr. Goodall personally thanked me when I had attended other events held by the Jane Goodall Institute of Canada, and as a result, I learned so much from this living legend and fascinating storyteller. Dr. Goodall spoke highly of the Roots and Shoots program as she continues to see how effective it is in building capacity to create a self-supporting community of leaders and educators. The Canadian Aboriginal Roots and Shoots Program is in the process of doing just that. She, like other environmentalists, strongly believes that indigenous peoples have the answers to many of our environmental issues, and so we should engage with and learn from them more.

The personal meetings I had with my mentor Dr. Jane Goodall were undoubtedly another great highlight of my career (Goodall 2010, 2011). After hearing that I was an anthropologist, she also shared with me her early experiences in the field. Her mentor, anthropologist Louis Leakey, sent her to study chimpanzees in Gombe National Park in Tanzania in 1960, and she only had secretarial experience, no training as a scientist or an anthropologist. She explained to me, "He wanted someone whose mind was not cluttered by scientific theory because back then ethology[10] was trying to become a very reductionistic hard science" (Goodall 2011). Dr. Goodall connected with the wisdom of an empathic approach to field research. She described how she became emotionally engaged with the chimpanzees, established relationships with them; and the qualitative data that emerged from her research has enriched the ethology of chimpanzees. When I asked how she deals with her critics that her work is not authentically scientific, she responded in an assertive tone that she remains unapologetic to her stern critics. "We can definitely have empathy and be objective at the same time—that is what science should be period."

Another great example of a community-driven process is how some indigenous communities have moved toward self-government. The 1996 Royal Commission on Aboriginal Peoples (RCAP) recommended that self-government be a critical part of renewing the nation-to-nation or government-to-government relationship based on four key principles: mutual recognition, mutual respect, mutual sharing and reciprocity, and mutual responsibility (RCAP 2011). However, RCAP did not elaborate on how self-government impacts the community (Ladner 2009). Aboriginal Affairs and Northern Development Canada conducted the Impact Assessment of Aboriginal Self-Government and Comprehensive Land Claims in 2003 and again in 2010, and it analyzed the impact of the well-being of self-governing Aboriginal communities (A. A. Canada 2014). The Impact Assessment found that between 1991 and 2006 employment levels for self-governing groups continued to improve. Specifically, self-governing communities experience a consistently lower unemployment rate than non-self-governed communities; self-governing communities have shown an increase in employment of 13.4 percent, while labor force participation grew by 12 percent. Chandler and Lalonde (2008), Papillon (2008), and Ladner (2009) all note how self-governance acts as a protective factor in suicide variability, community well-being, and resilience. These findings are in line with studies completed by both the World Bank and Harvard University[11] (A. A. Canada 2014). Ladner's (2009, 93) thorough review of literature also shows that there is a definitive correlation between self-determination and community well-being. Overall, the self-governed First Nation communities tend to have better education, employment, and labor force outcomes than those that remain under the Indian Act. Under the Indian Act, "the combination of stubborn federal funding arrangements and top-down programmatic demands and local pressures to resolve specific and persistent community problems has made the identification of program objectives and associated preferred outcomes difficult" (Shepherd and Persad 2011, 6). Thus, self-government agreements are an option for communities to move beyond the Indian Act, where Canada recognizes indigenous peoples' authorities from education to natural resource management (Irlbacher-Fox 2009). Self-government agreements are practical arrangements within the Canadian constitutional framework that recognize the authority of Aboriginal governments in areas that are internal and integral to their culture. The agreements establish government-to-government relationships that provide for jurisdictional clarity and address capacity and responsibilities for program and service delivery. They also address the structure and accountability of Aboriginal governments, their lawmaking powers, financial arrangements, and their responsibilities for providing programs and services to the community members. Many Aboriginal groups also seek to negotiate comprehensive land claim agreements leading to modern-day treaties, and these are formal undertakings between the Government of Canada, the provinces/territories, and Aboriginal peoples that provide certainty and clarity to ownership, use, and management of lands and resources. Such land claims help establish co-management regimes for lands, resources, and wildlife.

For example, in the Yukon, since 1990 when the Council of Yukon First Nations signed the Umbrella Final Agreement with the federal government, eleven of the fourteen First Nations in the region have signed and ratified their land claims agreement (Yukon Self-Government 2012). These eleven Yukon First Nation governments are no longer under the jurisdiction of the federal government's Indian Act. I recall a Yukon First Nation colleague of mine informing me that a distinct feature of the Yukon First Nation agreements is that they are inclusive and apply to everyone who considered themselves as part of their nation, not just "Status Indians," like most of the other agreements in Canada. Since 1973, Canada and Aboriginal groups have signed twenty-eight agreements, twenty of which include self-government provisions and three are stand-alone self-government agreements (A. A. Canada 2014). Currently, there are approximately ninety treaty and self-government negotiations in process. Nonetheless, there has not been as much take up of self-government as anticipated. The federal government is currently looking to implement a more results-based approach to treaty and self-government negotiations, as the goal is to conclude more agreements in less time for the benefit of all Canadians (A. A. Canada 2014). The self-government process is a complex, time-consuming process that is often not seen as responding to community pressures of the day. For many First Nations, it is quite challenging to leap from status-quo founded on the Indian Act to self-government. There are often many capacity challenges, and so many First Nations are not ready yet or do not have the infrastructure in place to address and resolve such challenges. They are faced with dismantling the structure of Band Councils imposed by the Indian Act, and this structure does not reflect the traditional governance systems that most indigenous peoples had in place before colonialism. Indigenous sovereignty, jurisdiction, laws, rules, and customs long predate contact with Europeans (Palmater 2014). Interestingly, Irlbacher-Fox (2009) contends that self-government negotiations tend to marginalize and exclude indigenous peoples' experiences and aspirations, where the agreement reached can unintentionally represent another iteration of colonization. Similar to Irbacher-Fox, Alfred (2009, 44) argues that increasing the material wealth or economic development in indigenous communities does not have a direct link to improving the people's overall well-being. "Throughout history, people that have overcome effects of colonization and recovered their dignity and regained the ability to be self-sufficient and autonomous have done so only after a sustained effort at spiritual revitalization and cultural regeneration" (Alfred 2009, 45). Thus, a fundamental and necessary process is the cultural revitalization that needs to occur for each indigenous community to heal and be ready to re-engage in and *own* their governance process; this process of decolonization can be a challenge in itself. Although the right of indigenous people to govern themselves was diminished as a result of colonialism, it was not extinguished (Penikett 2012), and therefore, the process is incremental as it may take time for a community to reconnect, re-empower, and resurge.

Because I, like Irlbacher-Fox, have adopted the cultural resurgence paradigm, as a bureaucrat involved on the policy side of self-government, I ensure that the indigenous community's vision, aspirations, and experiences are clearly articulated in the agreement as well as in the approval process. A responsible and accountable government can be achieved without dismantling the Indian Act by emphasizing self-determination (Ladner 2009, 93), as we have seen, for example, in Membertou First Nation in Nova Scotia[12] and Osoyoos First Nation in British Columbia.[13] Although self-government is not necessarily considered the same as self-determination in many communities, many indigenous negotiators view self-government agreements as one tool available among the many possibilities that may assist communities to achieve self-determination (Irlbacher-Fox 2009, 9). The concept of self-government, although seen as a federal government construct, is also considered as a process that provides "flexibility to develop innovative mechanisms consistent with the fundamental values, goals, and aspirations expressed through their communities' visions of self-determination" (Irlbacher-Fox 2009, 9). In fact, in my current position, in the Treaties and Aboriginal Government Sector, I ensure that a community's vision of self-determination is highlighted in our internal approval processes and placed in the forefront rather than reduced to a detail of the agreement process buried by government mechanisms and priorities. When I introduced this critical element to the interdepartmental meetings I chair, my fellow bureaucrats were initially surprised, but they soon realized how this enriches the process. It is so crucial for bureaucrats to acknowledge the community's vision as it is as critical if not more in the actual implementation of the agreement. In the end, it is important to recognize how a community defines how it comes together as a whole whether it is through self-government, a land claim agreement, or self-determination—in the end, it speaks to their resilience and their chosen, community-driven process of rebuilding, re-empowering their own constitutional orders and governance structures. What I have witnessed in many communities, as Ladner (2009, 98) also indicates, is that when indigenous peoples take control of their communities to decide and create how they want to govern themselves and live together, this can serve as the foundation for a community's healing journey. Community-based initiatives that allow the whole community to reconnect with the land, to preserve their culture and respectful ways of life tend to have lasting impact more so than a large-scale, self-government process.

Outside the Indian Act but short of the comprehensive land claims and self-government agreements, there are opportunities for First Nations to exercise jurisdiction through optional sectoral governance arrangements. These arrangements provide an opportunity to advance governance in specific areas, such as land management, oil and gas, financial administration, and education, and they can be a manageable and effective way to exercise self-governance broader than the incremental authority under the Indian Act (Parliament of Canada 1999). The disadvantages are that there is sometimes inconsistent jurisdiction, overlap, and confusion; however, the many First Nations I have met who have these arrangements in place feel that they really support their path toward self-government as they strengthen their capacity and readiness. In 1996, thirteen First Nations from British Columbia, Alberta, Saskatchewan, Manitoba, and Ontario signed a Framework Agreement with the federal government, which gave the First Nations control over reserve lands and resources. The legislation, namely the First Nation Land Management Act, was passed in 1999 to enable this sectoral agreement (Parliament of Canada 1999). In 1997, another sectoral agreement involved the transferring of the administrative jurisdiction on education to the nine Mi'kmaq First Nations, and the legislation, the Mi'kmaq Education Partnership with Nova Scotia, was passed in 1998.

Overall, with all the trials and tribulations, those communities that are self-governed, whether through a self-government process or another form of governance, exemplify a place-based approach, given that it all starts with the community coming together, with leadership on board both formal and informal like youth and Elders in the community, to develop a community plan based on its priorities and aspirations. A self-government agreement allows Aboriginal communities to contribute to and participate in the decisions that affect their lives and carry out effective relationships with other governments. Another example is the Crees in Quebec. Since the 1984 enactment of the Cree-Naskapi Act, the nine Cree communities of Quebec are no longer subject to the Indian Act (A. A. Canada 2014). As such, the Cree community governments and the Cree Regional Authority manage a land regime, participate in an environmental and social protection regime, and partner with various entities, such as the province of Quebec in economic development opportunities. The agreement is founded on the community's knowledge base, culture, assets, and collaborative networks. In this place-based approach, which is community driven, the community members "are not just sources of knowledge but active practitioners who coproduce new knowledge that remains rooted in the communities of which they are a part" (Davidson-Hunt and O'Flaherty 2007, 297).

As seen in self-governed communities and in youth-led community projects, factors for success in such place-based approaches include linking knowledge clusters and assets in the community, creating new relationships through collaboration, and creating and re-creating knowledge legacy through a revitalized and expanded body of knowledge. As there are limitations with conventional research and policy development, there are limitations with place-based approach if undertaken in isolation without dialogic networks with external partners. Although Canada and the United States have seen examples of innovation and progress in designing and implementing place-based policy, focusing on leveraging local assets for better national outcomes, the many initiatives are insufficiently aligned, and learning opportunities have been missed (Bradford 2005). What is required as well is a rethinking and retooling process especially with respect to moving from a centralized government (top-down process) to a lens on local governance, where local voices are valued. This paradigm emphasizes the identification and mobilization of endogenous potential of communities, which include essentially the human capital and innovative capacities and assets (Tomaney 2010). "Local and regional development is a global challenge, but one which requires locally fashioned responses" (Tomaney 2010, 12). Place-based is not an alternative approach to federal policies, but it requires a shift in the government's approach in that it becomes an enabler in the development of community-based strategies and solutions. The government can try to better facilitate, orchestrate, and harness the external resources necessary to support community-driven processes. Also, there should not be the sole focus on local or community in isolation of other communities. The connections or networks with neighboring communities, cities (if applicable), provinces, or territories in Canada are critical in shaping their process and success.

T'SOUKE FIRST NATION COMMUNITY

A First Nation community in British Columbia comes to mind. When I visited T'Souke[14] First Nation, I was given a tour of the self-governing community of 251 members, which had undergone the development of a comprehensive community plan, and the chief and his community led their plan to full implementation and success. T'Souke is considered as Canada's most solar intensive community (T'Souke Nation 2013). T'Souke began its journey to become a sustainable solar community with a comprehensive community planning process that involved everyone, including children. The guiding principle for the planning was based on the Seventh Generation, planning one hundred years ahead. They engaged in mapping their assets, exploring their land and its resources, and each member had a role and a voice. The T'Souke Nation realized that in order to achieve sustainability, it needed to embrace traditional values including deep respect for Mother Earth (T'Sou-ke Nation 2013). A large solar panel was developed within the community, and they are now selling back hydro-electricity to neighboring cities in the area. In order to produce electricity, large photovoltaic systems were installed above and beside the community's canoe shed. Solar hot water systems were installed in forty houses, and a comprehensive energy conservation program took place. Ten members of the community received training in installing solar hot water systems and worked with contractors in placing those systems on half the houses on the reserve and in the community kitchen. The entire community got involved in energy conservation initiatives when T'Souke discovered that it costs just one-tenth the price to save energy as it does to produce it. An unexpected side benefit of the T'Souke solar project was that the nation created a unique eco-tourism program. When solar installations were completed in 2009, T'Souke invited all levels of government and First Nations to a weekend gathering with much dancing and drumming, solar tours and workshops. This year alone, T'Souke has had many schools, municipalities and tourists from all over the world come for tours and workshops (T'Souke Nation 2013). T'Souke also developed a greenhouse project and a successful community garden, which has been named the Ladybug Garden, where they harvest greens and vegetables. The garden brings youth and Elders together, and the youth go on outings with Elders in the bush for lessons on edible and medicinal plants and medicinal teas and what they are or were used for in the past. The woman whom I met and who gave me the tour of the garden shared that "a portion of the produce from the garden, like berries, beans, peas, and greens is distributed to Elders or used by our community cooks for either meals on wheels, community lunches or cultural nights. This creates self-sufficiency within our community." At the end of her presentation, she gave me a jar of their local blackberry jam that they had just made. The community is currently working closely with the province's greenhouse industry, as well as with the universities in the province to both inform and learn from their partners. In particular, they are working toward the development of a First Nations agricultural database to help promote new initiatives and support community-based business ventures (T'Souke Nation 2013).

T'Souke demonstrates how renewable energy, which is unique to their "place," can unite a community, strengthen cultural connections, and secure economic development opportunities for long-term sustainability. This case also speaks to how the form and nature of the place of the community can shape people's life chances, and the relationships to social capital through formal and informal networks are fundamental to implementation and sustainability. The success that T'Souke First Nation is experiencing has much to do with the dialogic networks they have developed with both internal members of the community and external partners, from academia, governments, and industries. I strongly believe that what is required to move forward in the area of policy development is more of collaboration between two paradigms, the formal government approach, and the grassroots, place-based approach. In this way, policy development becomes a two-way translation process where the synergy between formal research and tacit, experiential knowledge is maximized. This reciprocal process involves "on the one hand breaking down and re-working formal research so that it can be applied to specific practical contexts and, on the other, articulating the practitioner insights and know-how so that these can be shared as formal knowledge" (Leviten-Reid 2004, 8). As in T'Souke First Nation, both researchers, government officials, and indigenous people are collaborators in the process of knowledge production—the people are considered creative co-authors in research and policy development. This is how we decolonize the policy world and research relationships, where the knowledge and values of indigenous people are valued equally to the science-based perspectives of researchers (Davidson-Hunt and O'Flaherty 2007), and new knowledge is co-produced by this dialogic network founded on trust, respect, and partnerships. I have noted in many cases where the First Nations are viewed as resourceful experts rather than the researchers or government officials alone, and they are all working together as colleagues.

In my experience, the challenges lie with overcoming our own cultural assumptions, especially how Western academia is more valid than indigenous scholarship and how it is implied that government officials have more expertise and knowledge than indigenous peoples. I believe the most effective way to rethink this assumption is to not validate the authority of indigenous scholarship over Western thinking but rather to create intersections, bridges between the two, to enrich each domain. There is a growing appreciation of the complementarity that exists between what were previously considered two disparate and irreconcilable systems of thought (Barnhardt and Kawagley 2005). Another related cultural assumption in the federal government policy world is how a given policy can be seen as a static construct produced to accommodate the federal, corporate authority. Too often, we as policy creators become so engulfed in feeding the federal system, we do not realize we are developing policy under the anaesthetic of corporate influence (White 1996, 14). We need to step back and reflect that policies have "important economic, legal, cultural and moral implications" (Shore and Wright 1997, 7), as they are cultural texts, rhetorical devices, and discursive formations that can empower some and silence others (Shore and Wright 1997; Wedel and Feldman 2005). As a governance tool and cultural agent, a policy has direct implications on individuals and their lived realities, and so it is impossible to ignore its influence. We need to reconfigure how knowledge is shared and power is produced and focus on building the relationship between the global and the local, and illuminate how organizational worlds and people's realities are interconnected (Wedel and Feldman 2005). In 2011, I was involved in creating a network with the Crees and Inuit of the Hudson Bay region, the Government of Nunavut, provincial government, non-governmental organizations, the private sector, and academia. This network, namely the Hudson Bay Inland Sea Initiative (HBISI) is working together to more effectively plan for the future of environmental stewardship for the greater Hudson Bay watershed and ecosystem. The Crees and Inuit living along the Hudson Bay are experiencing the effects of climate change and their adaptation entails reconnecting with and applying their traditional knowledge of local ecosystems leading to potential solutions.[15] For over 20 years, the Crees and Inuit have expressed concerns regarding the cumulative impact of hydroelectric development on the marine environment. The toxic pollutants from this development have threatened the resilience of the ecosystem and the people dependent on it (Benoit 2011). The HBISI exemplifies how building a bridge between government and local voices, and scientific and traditional knowledges informs the policy development process in hopes to create locally meaningful policies. This initiative will support the development of an inter-jurisdictional governance or networked governance, where the vision of environmental stewardship as well as accountability and responsibility are shared among the stakeholders and various levels of government (Benoit 2011, 18).

As illustrated in this chapter, the corporate, federal network and the network of people in communities living through the implications of policies should be interwoven and not isolated from each other and so should work together from the initial phase of policy development so that the rhetorical discourse created reflects the ongoing dialogue among all involved. The progress in indigenous communities has been more incremental than anticipated, and I believe it partly has to do with the federal government learning to undo and deconstruct their authoritative gaze to more effectively support community-driven processes. It is part of the rethinking process we need to engage in, and each public servant involved in supporting indigenous communities in whatever shape or form should listen and learn from our indigenous partners and scholars, and become more personally engaged. Essentially, this entails engaging our indigenous partners, community members, formal and informal leaders as creative, valuable coauthors in the policy-making process. The more we as policy creators network and build more effective working relationships with our indigenous partners, the more we decrease the risk of unintended consequences, and the better we engage in decolonizing the policy world. As will be further explored in chapter 6, citizen engagement is a critical principle to cultural competence.

NOTES

1. For a more elaborate illustration of Tom's art therapy experience see Ferrara (2004).

2. In many First Nation communities, comprehensive community planning, has been quite successful. Some refer to it as community-based community planning but all have the underlying goal of community-driven plan that promotes local leadership and inclusion of all members, and it speaks to the community's vision of its development.

3. Prior to the *Interest Group for the Anthropology of Public Policy* (Feldman and Wedel 2004) was the Committee on Public Policy within the American Anthropological Association (AAA), which was established in 1998, and its internal mission is to develop public policy expertise and enhance public policy debate among anthropologists through workshops and public policy forum (AAA 2009). The Committee's external mission is to highlight the salience of anthropologists' efforts in working with policy makers and other organizations. The Committee is also dedicated to educating policy makers on issues where anthropological expertise can be brought to bear (AAA 2009).

4. This model for describing health determinants emphasizes interactions among the layers of influence on health. Individual lifestyles are embedded within social norms and networks, and living and working conditions, which in turn are related to the wider socioeconomic and cultural environment (Dahlgren and Whitehead 1991).

5. Environmentalist, David Suzuki told a group of First Nations leaders that obsession with economic development will lead to a "dead end" for the planet and First Nations people can help educate others about sustainability and that we can all benefit from lessons on the environment from First Nations (http://www.thestarphoenix.com/life/Take+enviro+lessons+from+First+Nations+environmentalist/9074534/story.html).

6. Many policy analysts tend to minimize this role as knowledge broker and not recognize the value as communities do. From the community's perspective, having an external partner to help the community connect the dots is invaluable as a resource.

7. A Comprehensive Community Plan (CCP) addresses all different pieces that make up life in a healthy, successful community—land, economic development, health and well-being, housing, language and culture. CCP is viewed by many First Nations as a valuable tool to guide decisions for sustainable living and a healthy environment. A community plan is inspired by the aspirations, dreams, and the vision of community members and also based on thorough understanding of local history and present conditions (Lac La Ronge 2012). A CCP is considered a process more than a product including various stages, such as preplanning, planning, implementation, monitoring, and evaluation. It is process driven, designed, and implemented by the community for the community.

8. The community plan can be viewed at www.azaccp.ca.

9. www.janegoodall.ca/WisdomKeepersStorytellerVideos.php.

10. Ethology is the study of animal behavior with emphasis on the behavioral patterns that occur in natural environments.

11. The Harvard Project on American Indian Economic Development's (2010) analysis of successful economic development of Native American tribes determined that the critical factors for economic success are sovereignty, culture, administrative ability, and leadership. The Harvard Project noted the direct correlation between good governance and economic success, which are necessary to provide for community well-being, create resilience, and address the conditions that enable or disable communities in crisis (Ladner 2009, 94).

12. The Membertou First Nation provides a very good example of how leaders can stimulate the entrepreneurial spirit within their communities, and create the environment that fosters socioeconomic development. The elements of good governance, leadership and vision, transparency and accountability are hallmarks of International Organization of Standardization (ISO 9001) certification, which Membertou obtained in 2001, becoming the first indigenous community in the world (Membertou First Nation 2014). Membertou is an ideal example of what it takes to transform a community in crisis to one that is an exemplar of good governance and resilience.

13. The Osoyoos First Nation efforts to reduce dependency and attain self-sufficiency began in 1988 with the establishment of the Osoyoos Indian Band Development Corporation. Osoy-

oos owns a successful golf course that has had a multimillion dollar expansion, and it also operates a sawmill in collaboration with a U.S. company. The community formed a partnership with Vincor, the largest wine producer in Canada, which leases 800 acres from the Osoyoos for grape production. The community's focus of their economic development and nation building is through preserving their cultural heritage (Governance 2013).

14. T'Souke is pronounced as "Sooke"—the former is the First Nation original name for the community, and the latter is the English name that settlers had used. T'Souke is from the Senchoten (Sen-cho-sen) dialect of the Northern Straits Salish family, and it refers to the name of the Stickleback fish that live in the river that runs alongside the community.

15. For more information, see http://arcticeider.com/en/knowledge-solutions.

Chapter Five

Personal Lived Reality

Opening of My Self

Throughout my studies, my career as a therapist, as an academic, and now as a bureaucrat, the message was clear to refrain from referring to one's self as this would threaten the realm of objectivity, which is considered so much more paramount than subjectivity. Our voice is to remain passive as subjectivity has no place in science. What is also quite evident is a refrain from reflexivity as a method of discovery. This refrain nurtured my personal challenge to demonstrate the value of subjectivity and the practice of reflexivity. I have consciously worked at deconstructing this unnecessary dichotomy—that is, objectivity versus subjectivity—and to highlight the importance of self-reflexivity in clinical work, in anthropology, in research, and in policy development.[1] I desperately sought a theoretical framework that validates reflection as a method of discovery because I hoped there were others out there that thought the same way or valued reflection/subjectivity as I did. Intersubjectivity permeates my everyday life and career, and intersubjectivity and reflexivity provide an opening of the self that avoids turning ourselves and those we work with into static and mummified objects (Salzman 2002, 807; Bhabha 1994). To deny the voice of an individual, my own, and that of another is to deny humanity, and to devalue intersubjectivity and what we gain from both inter- and intradialogue also devalues humanity. Reflexivity in research is a process of critical reflection both on how knowledge is produced from research and how knowledge is generated. It involves a continuous process of critical scrutiny and interpretation and allows a researcher to focus on subjectivity in an inescapably intimate way (Bucholtz 2001). Bucholtz further elaborates, "We don't just think things about research, we don't just believe them—we feel them, and we need to explore the profound consequences of that fact" (Bucholtz 2001, 181–182). The drive for reflexivity also supports the process of decolonization as the more we learn, we listen, we demystify, and we deconstruct our cultural assumptions. If we are social scientists working with other humans, then it only makes sense to value the role of reflexivity. In humanistic inquiry and ethnography, reflection is a way of ensuring rigor and ethical practice (Guillemin and Gillam 2004), and it is a moral methodological necessity. Any rejection of subjective experience entails a deeply troubling inattention to individuals' lives as lived (Desjarlais and Throop 2011, 96). As La Barré (1967, ix) stated clearly and this remains quite relevant today, "the un-self-examined anthropologist . . . has no right or business anthropologizing," and I would extend this to the clinician, researcher, and policy analyst. Once ethical dimensions are inherent in any practice, it necessitates integrating processes of self-reflection rather than segregating moral judgments from practices (Holdsworth and Morgan 2007, 406). As mentioned in chapter 1, in therapy as in the field, denying the value of reflexivity promotes countertransference and leads to blurred understandings and, moreover, results in a disservice to both the informants and to the ethnographer's own self-growth (cf. Spiro 1996). If the subjectivity of the informants and ethnographer are ignored or mismanaged, it becomes, as Devereux (1967, 202) contends "a real source of sterile error." To me, it is clear that without self-reflection, decolonization cannot be fully realized.

ETHNOHERMENEUTICS AND INTERSUBJECTIVITY

Similar to dialogical anthropology is the approach of ethnohermeneutics, which "attempts to locate both the researcher and human subjects in each of their net of texts, traditions, meanings, and social and intellectual circumstances" (A. Geertz, 2003, 311). This approach, as in hermeneutical analysis, places the analyst and the subject on equal terms with each other. As I treated my patients as partners in the healing process, I treat my indigenous colleagues as partners in the reconciliation process rather than objects of my work (Biehl, Good, and Kleinman, 2007). In a similar vein, the approach in reflexive anthropology "is rooted in the premise that ethnographic fieldwork is an intersubjective process that entails an interaction of various subjectivities" (Jacobs-Huey, 2002, 791). I found resonance in A. W. Geertz's approach on ethnohermeneutics and his study of the Hopi Indian religion because of its tenet that interpretations are also reflections of the scholar, and where the frames of reference of the scholar and the people under study transcend. Geertz (2003) argues that as analysts we must be aware of our own horizons of understanding. As researchers, we need to critically consider our own cultural identity, our own cultural biases especially when engaging in the translation of other cultures and other voices. As I learned from Luke early on in my career, it is all about respectful reciprocity and mutual reflection, and this is valued by the indigenous people I work with, and most of the time, what is appreciated is "old fashioned courtesy and openness" (Geertz 1994, 4). A Cree Elder I currently work closely with told me: "If you are going to build trust, the only way to do it is to be truthful from the start. Don't hide behind fancy words—just be clear with your intentions." Anthropologists, scholars, public servants too often use terminology to demonstrate their professional competence. As Wikan (2012, 118) contends: "Little is gained by making distinctions, creating concepts that blind us to people's lived predicaments." Perhaps within their inner circle such jargon makes sense, but oftentimes it distances us from the people we are working with. The reality is we are working with and learning from other human beings and learning about ourselves. We cannot escape the fact that our discipline is about human experience. Rather than to claim that anthropology has lost its center (Appell 1992) because of its struggle with defining itself as a scientific inquiry, I think we need to redefine, rethink its center, and accept and appreciate that anthropology has at its core a humanistic inquiry that enriches and complements science rather than opposes it. We should take pride in our discipline because of this reality, because of its unique quality to allow humans to make sense of their lived realities with other humans, to provide an avenue of expression of rich narratives, illustrating perceptions of interpersonal, intercultural experiences and dialogue. Whatever theoretical framework or jargon selected, the end result is an ethnographic account, a story articulated by the unique stance of the author and his or her unique experiences in the field, an account of "the existential richness of people's lives" (Desjarlais and Throop 2011, 96). I, too, like Throop (2003), believe that our ethnographic accounts dictate our theoretical frameworks.

In my very fortunate encounters with Professor Jean Briggs in 2000, she was adamant that the objective of anthropology should be to attain intersubjective understanding. She was concerned with anthropologists not including themselves in their ethnographies because as she noted, "in so doing, they are alienating themselves. It is quite unfortunate for both them and the people they are studying" (Briggs 2000). According to Briggs, the nature of fieldwork is both dialogic and intersubjective. It resonated with me as we were both working in indigenous communities. She talked extensively about how Inuit children were socialized (for example, how children were socialized to suppress their anger) and how she would naturally react to what she considered different, but in discussing her observations with her informants, and sharing her thoughts, reactions, it helped her develop a better understanding of their cultural ways of parenting. The more she talked, inquired, or reacted, the more she learned to appreciate the differences. As I had also experienced with the Inuit in particular, Briggs's openness and transparency with her feelings, thoughts, and her readiness to learn was deeply appreciated. As "[i]t is through our intellectual readiness, coupled with exposure to a wide range of experience, that we create a sense of lived experience—ours and others" (Fine and Deegan 1996, 445).

OPENING MY SELF — A SERENDIPITOUS AND TRANSFORMATIVE EXPERIENCE

Anthropological research is a lifelong nomadic journey of discovery, and ethnographic fieldwork demands a combination of empathy, objectivity, as well as subjectivity (Hazan and Hertzog 2012). It entails an adaptation to a fluid world, and the significance goes beyond the boundaries of ethnography. I will further highlight with a personal, transformative experience. It was an early evening in later August in an Ojibwe-Cree community in the sub-Arctic. I was invited to engage in an annual, week-long youth gathering to help support their healing process. The Elders asked that I join them at the fire pit, drink tea, and just be.[2] During the days that preceded this, I had worked closely with the Elders and we got to know each other quite well. At this circle of gathering, some shared their personal stories about the past, hunting, life in the bush, how they would predict the weather (and they bragged how they were always accurate!), residential schools, their grand-children, and the future of their communities. There were many moments of silence that were so appreciated by all as we needed to absorb what was being shared. After some time had passed, Irene, an Elder looked straight at me and said, "You are a healer, you know," as she nodded with confidence. I sat there astounded, and I recall looking around the circle and noticing the other Elders nodding in agreement. Suddenly, I felt like I was in a liminal state, a place of transition, absorbing the environment, the people, and the expressions, both verbal and nonverbal. It was subtle yet profound mirroring of the words of the Elder. I experienced what Bhabha (1994, 60) refers to as "the elliptical *in-between*, where the shadow of the other falls upon the self" (emphasis by author), in that the focus shifted from me observing them to them focused on me. This was an unexpected, serendipitous event, and the natural environment I was in was conducive to creating an experience laden with meaning, defined by self-transformation and maturity. It was an emotional, spiritual, physical, and sensual lived experience as I recall the distinct scents, the taste of the hot tea, the sound of the wind, and the crackling fire, the smell of the firewood and the surrounding pine trees, and that evening, for the first time in my life, I saw the sky filled with the aurora borealis. This life chance empowered me and allowed me to reconnect with my inner potential that I had suppressed for so long. At the same time, I felt like my vulnerability was exposed, and I felt like "a naked anthropologist" (DeVita

1991, xvi), given that I found myself in a situation where I learned something that I had not been trained or prepared for, which derived from serendipity rather than from the practice of social science. As I remained in shock and took time to process what had just happened, Irene said: "You need to continue working with our people, in our communities, but you also need to bring your healing to your own community." I promised Irene and the other Elders that I would follow through. I was honored by this gift and the title I was granted, and so I felt morally responsible to act on my promise.

Within a month, I drafted a proposal to open a mental health clinic, and I brought it to the Director General of an Italian-based community hospital, which happened to be the hospital where I was born. In my presentation of the proposal, I recall presenting it with confidence. The treatment of a patient's mental and spiritual well-being was gravely overlooked. I referred to my grandmother and my aunt who had passed away in the palliative care unit at the hospital and how they and the family had no mental health support. I was told, "Many Italian immigrants will not respond to psychotherapy. It is highly stigmatized." I convinced her that it was worth trying, and I reassured her that I would work with the team of doctors and not in isolation to offer a more comprehensive treatment for each patient in oncology and palliative care. The following week I started working in the oncology unit. I worked closely with the oncologists, and they thought that the services I was to offer their patients was timely and so necessary as it filled in a critical gap in the patient's overall treatment. I ended up following each patient from initial diagnosis to palliative care, and I treated the family members as well. Many of my patients were drawn to creating a life review using a photo journal, and oftentimes, they would request that I, on their behalf, transfer their journal to their loved ones when they would near their death while in palliative care. As the word spread that this service was now available to patients, once again in my career as a clinician, my waiting list kept getting longer and longer. At times, I had to limit the intake to patients in oncology and palliative care because it became overwhelming as I was receiving referrals from emergency room doctors, surgeons, and other specialists.

MISTAKES LEADING TO INSIGHTS

One day at the hospital, a man in his early forties was referred to me for a psychological assessment and treatment by a doctor in the trauma emergency room. The man was on the brink of personal bankruptcy, he was in an extreme depressed state, and he had just attempted suicide. I had a small office space in the hospital, and when he entered, the room was engulfed with a poignant and repulsive body odor. Trying desperately to remain focused, I painstakingly kept trying to open the window but to no avail while this man was expressing his profound emotions and crying. He expressed how he felt at ease talking to me, and at the end of the session he asked to see me again. At the end of the session, I gave him false hope in agreeing to see him again. However, knowing I would not be able to stomach the body odor, I informed my assistant to refer him to a psychologist at another clinic. I assumed he would return with the same dishevelled look and lack of personal hygiene. When he had called in to schedule his appointment, he insisted he wanted to see me, but my assistant told him he was being referred to see another psychologist. That same week, I found out he was brought in by paramedics who had found him dead in his home. He had committed suicide. As a clinician, I viewed this as a failure on my part. I could have tried to work around what I viewed as an obstacle to my responsiveness. I could have been more attentive, more tolerant, and more empathic, but I was not. At a cognitive, rational level, I am aware that I did not cause his suicide, but what I do know is that by not validating him during his most vulnerable state, that that could have been a trigger to his suicide. I agree with Kent (1991, 23) that it is through failures as well as successes that we learn about being human. Through this failure, I gained insight and a more in-depth understanding of rejection. I learned about myself through this individual. This experience allowed me to reconnect with my personal experience of being rejected. I reconnected with this aspect of my vulnerability. As a result of this experience, my empathy heightened for my next patient, and more importantly, I found ways to better adapt and cope with my idiosyncrasies that could become obstacles.

Soon after, I received another referral of a fifty-eight-year-old woman, whom I will refer to as Pauline, who had recently been admitted in oncology. When I arrived at the nursing station to start my rounds, the nurse asked if the doctor who had given me this referral had debriefed me. I said no as I prefer meeting the patients before reading their file or hearing from their doctor. She raised her eyebrows, wished me good luck and directed me to the room this patient was in. When I walked in, there was a man sitting by her bedside yelling at her. I ignored him and focused on this woman who was holding tightly onto her bed sheets up to her neck. She looked at me, and she began talking while he, her boyfriend, kept raising his voice telling her to "show the doctor what you did to yourself, you idiot!" I asked him to step outside, but he refused so I told her I was there for her and to listen to her story. As she was talking, I couldn't help but notice a blood stain increasing in size on the bed sheet she kept grasping onto. I shared this with her as he yelled out, "Show her what you did!" I thought that maybe she had a wound that needed to be redressed. Pauline lowered the sheet and revealed a large cavity, filled with live maggots, surrounding her heart muscle. I blinked several times in disbelief, and then reality hit and my whole being started shaking. As I held onto the bedrail and absorbed what I had just seen, I remained focused on Pauline's eyes. Her boyfriend finally stepped out of the room, and she covered her chest again. I asked if she wanted me to call the nurse, and she replied, "Please don't leave. I need to talk to you." With a calm voice and heavy breathing she told me about her life in Belgium and that she came from a wealthy family. She was unhappily married for many years, and so she decided to leave her husband to much dismay of family and friends. She was a millionaire but very unhappy with her husband. When she decided to leave her husband, she was shamed by family and friends for doing so. Her only daughter pleaded that she remain in Belgium, but Pauline had fallen in love with this Canadian man and decided to move to Canada to escape the shame and judgment she was experiencing. As a result, her relationship with her daughter was severed. Pauline began crying and telling me she thought she would be happier with this man but realized all he wanted was her money. She said she did not leave him because she got really ill and weak, and so she told herself it was better to have someone there than to be completely alone. Pauline had been diagnosed with aggressive breast cancer, but she refused medical treatment and decided to treat her cancer with homeopathic remedies. When she was brought into emergency, she was ashamed of her open chest cavity and so kept her purse close to it in order not to expose it.[3] At our subsequent sessions, she realized her condition was deteriorating and she did not have much time left. She pleaded for me to help contact her daughter. Her last wish was to speak to her and ask for her forgiveness. Later that day, Pauline went into a coma. My staff and I worked on locating her daughter in Belgium, and when we did, I gave her a call. We spoke for a while, and she explained how her mother was a woman with such grace and dignity and she was so sad to hear of her present condition. I informed her daughter that Pauline was in a coma as her organs were shutting down and her condition was deteriorating quickly. I recall telling her that her mom still exuded that grace and dignity and that her last wish was to speak to her only daughter. She agreed to speak to her mom. I held Pauline's hand, told her that her daughter was on the phone, and placed it to her ear. Pauline shed tears, and moments after, she gave out her last breath. When I took the phone to speak to her daughter, she told me she told her mom she loved her and forgave her and that it was time to go in peace. I informed her that she had just given her last breath. The daughter cried uncontrollably but later expressed that she too was at peace for having granted her mom's last wish. Personally, this was another transformative experience of witnessing the power of the human spirit, its resilience, and its grace.

CREATING INTERSECTIONS BETWEEN EXPERIENCES

I continued to work in indigenous communities while holding my clinic at
the hospital and teaching undergraduate anthropology courses at both McGill
and Concordia Universities. Because I brought my experiential knowledge
from one field experience to another, I created linkages that benefited both
my indigenous patients and Euro-Canadian ones by tapping into my experiential knowledge and drawing from it what would be considered relevant in
treating each patient. My knowledge base proved as heuristic. I will illustrate
further with a case. Peter, a fifty-one-year-old man of French Canadian descent, was a patient of mine in oncology, and he was being treated for
pancreatic cancer. His oncologist told him he had a few months to live. Peter
experienced ambivalence about his inevitable death, at times embracing it
and at other times, fearing it, feeling it all being unfair because he felt he had
so much left to do. In our sessions, he created a photo journal highlighting his
meaningful life events, and he had a writing journal. Peter had also prepared
a bucket list, which he carried with him wherever he went. His top, number
one wish was to share his insights with a large audience.

Given that I was also teaching at the universities, I organized a lecture
where Peter was the guest speaker in one of my anthropology courses. It was
quite timely as I scheduled his presentation when narrative discourse was on
the course agenda. The students were asked to read some chapters from
Kleinman (1988) and Ochs and Capps (2001). How best to further elaborate
on narrative discourse theory than through an individual's expression of his
life narrative. He talked about the insights he gained as a tree cutter for a
hydroelectric company. He said he treated the trees with respect and he
would trim them ensuring he did not harm the trees. He felt responsible for
the trees. Peter shared his written narratives and his poetry with the students.
The students showed interest in hearing more about his passion, his life, and
how he was coping with his illness. He spoke for the full two hours, and he
was completely engaged and engaging. Peter ended his lecture with a pas-
sionate plea for the students to be open minded, open and respectful toward
others, nature, and life and mortality. He thanked the students wholehearted-
ly for listening to him and at the end, as he shed tears, he told them that what
he just did was a dream come true for him and it meant more to him than they
will ever know. Peter then thanked me for granting his wish. Both the students and Peter were ambivalent about saying goodbye that evening. One
student asked if Peter would return again because he wanted to hear and learn
more from Peter and his insights. Peter was honest with the students and
expressed how he knew his condition was deteriorating, and so as much as he
would have liked to return, he knew he most likely would be too weak. He
shared copies of his insights that he had recently written in one of our sessions. He had asked me to make copies to give to the students as he wanted to

ensure his message was well conveyed and remembered. As he shed tears, he told the students, "I feel like my story is unfinished." Peter, similar to Capps in the eloquent last chapter of *Living Narrative* (Ochs and Capps 2001), exemplified how some stories will never have a comprehensive end.

I had shared some aspects of Cree and Mohawk cosmologies with Peter about how we should rethink our attachment to the environment, to the land. Peter expressed how the values attached to nature resonated with him as he said that he felt connected to every tree he climbed and trimmed. He too believed that he was a steward of the land, and for him, the trees in particular. What Peter had also adopted in particular from my experiential knowledge and experience with indigenous peoples was that we come from the earth and return back when we die. This made complete sense to him because of how he had embodied his experience with trees, and this also brought him a sense of serenity and helped him accept his death. At our next sessions, he grew weaker and weaker and eventually was brought to me in a wheelchair. He reached out and showed me his bucket list and thanked me for enabling him to check off his "dream to speak to a group of people." Peter died a month later in his home surrounded by his loved ones, which was his last wish.

What I learned from my clinical experience with my patients in oncology and palliative care benefitted my work with my indigenous patients. I shared with my indigenous patients who were experiencing suicidal ideation, and some who had experienced actual attempts, how many of my Euro-Canadian patients, those of Italian origin in particular, showed a profound attachment to their cultural identity, and used this connection in their healing process. While treating my indigenous patients, I would often refer to my work with Euro-Canadian patients and share how they would express the importance of their families, their customs, and their language. When they felt disconnected, there was often a strong need to reconnect with their cultural identity and this was a notion that had significant resonance with my indigenous patients. Such strong and meaningful values helped them sustain their sense of belongingness especially when they felt isolated and alone in their illness experience. Sharing this helped many of my indigenous patients realize that they too can try to do the same; however, it was important to consider that my indigenous patients had experienced cultural oppression where my Euro-Canadian ones had not. Nonetheless, this intersection from one patient's experience and personal narratives to another proved to be effective in many cases.

LIFE NARRATIVES

With both my Euro-Canadian and indigenous patients, my focus was rarely on capturing their illness narratives (Kleinman 1988) and more on their personal life stories (Wikan 2012). Like Peacock and Holland (1993, 377), I view life storytelling as central to human existence. My view has been nurtured by my own cultural exposure, especially from my grandparents, to the value placed on storytelling as well as by the indigenous cosmologies I have been exposed to where oral tradition is so closely linked to one's individual and collective existence. My grandfathers in particular believed that stories are windows on our experiences, psyche, and soul (Peacock and Holland 1993). They both shared their stories with pride, and they knew they were sharing pieces of their individual selves and their cultural identity. As they grew older, there was a heightened sense of urgency to share their stories to ensure we would not forget them. The message was made clear to listen while they spoke because as much as the story they would share was a reflection of their life experience, we would learn from them as well. My grandparents and my patients exemplified how a life story or personal narrative is definitely a fundamental means of making sense of experience, and narratives help give form to experience (Ochs and Capps 1996, 19; Ochs and Capps 2001). It was a critical aspect of their healing process to grant primacy and validity to my patients' stories that spoke about their realities and aspirations (Kirmayer, Guzder, and Rousseau 2014). With my patients, discourse was multidimensional where narratives transformed through the expression, the actual telling of their stories, whether through the two- or three-dimensional art expression or their written pieces. Many of my cancer patients used writing journals and created photo albums to express their life stories.

As social scientists, we should not reduce life stories to a status of anecdotal as they offer a methodologically privileged focal point from which to comprehend an individual life trajectory. Maynes, Pierce, and Laslett (2008), two sociologists and a historian, effectively interweave the connections among individual agency, historically and socially embedded processes of self-construction, and the culturally specific narrative forms in which individuals construct their life stories and subjectivities. Other scholars, such as Mishler (1999), Bell (2004), Atkinson and Delamont (2006), and Mattingly (2006) to name a few, have applied personal narrative analysis in their research, demonstrating that the unease and suspicion about the value of life histories is gradually decreasing (Maynes et al. 2008). In Portelli's (1991, 130) interdisciplinary approach to oral history, he makes a critical point: "The fact that a culture is made up of individuals different from one another is one of the important things that social sciences sometimes forget, and of which oral history reminds us." Interestingly, this methodological framework of personal narrative analysis mirrors many indigenous epistemologies and the value placed on narratives and oral history. How an individual's life course is influenced by cultural and collective histories has been embedded in indigenous cosmologies since time immemorial. What is also commonly understood is that personal narratives are created through interpersonal and intersubjective relationships.

Personal narratives involve an intersubjective understanding (Maynes et al. 2008). Portelli (1991, 130) also claims that "an oral speech act . . . is implicitly social because it requires an audience." While it is a self-expression created by the individual, it is also an expression of the sharing between the narrator and interlocutor, who is listening to the narrator. The narrative is an expression of the sharing of one's personal experiences with another (Levy 2005), therefore, an expression of the intersubjective encounter. In the narrative construction and reconstruction, existential negotiations between the listener and the narrator occur (Mattingly 1994). Meaning is generated from the expression of the narrative, the dynamics of the relationship between the teller and the listener, and the narrative itself. The value of the narrative is critical in a human-oriented, life-focused approach (Peacock and Holland 1993) to healing as well as in medical anthropology. The narratives I was exposed to were not just about the illness or whatever condition the individual was experiencing; however, the illness does act as a catalyst and the narratives do flow more rapidly and urgently in times of crisis (Levy 2005).

In both clinical experiences, I witnessed how reconnecting with memory has a healing quality as it is critical when retrieving and narrating life experiences. In self-construction overall or in the healing process in particular, we cannot deny the fundamental power of narrative. It is connected to the creation of self and the sharing of self with others (Levy 2005). What is of equal importance is the role of life chances, contingencies, and human to human interactions that influence the form and expression of the narrative. There definitely is therapeutic value in rediscovering one's self, whether it is individual or collective self-identity (cf. Niezen 2009) through expressions of personal life stories, through interactions with nature and with other humans (Ferrara 2004). Moreover, there is significant value in listening to another person's life stories as they have definitely contributed to my own personal growth, enhancing my skills as a healer as well as a policy creator. For the reasons outlined above, I believe personal life stories need to be in the forefront of human sciences not in anomalous isolation (Peacock and Holland 1993).

FACING MY FEARS

I could have chosen any other area to start up a mental health clinic, but after much reflection as well as guidance from my Elders, I chose to face my fear of mortality and try to resolve my issues with such finality. I was socialized to view death as a dramatic ending, a very unbalanced view where all my weight was on the grief, loss, and emptiness. It was forbidden to celebrate the individual's life, and I recall when my grandfather died, my cousins and I (ages between four and fifteen) started laughing, and this was so frowned upon and we were immediately reprimanded. We were socialized to fear death, and then when some of my family members were diagnosed with cancer, it was interpreted as a death sentence even if it was not a severe form of cancer. I saw the same in my Italian patients in oncology and more so with them than with my other Euro-Canadian patients. I was nine years old when my grandfather died, and it traumatized me to a point of me becoming an insomniac because I would wait up for him as he had promised me he would never leave me. When I soon realized he wasn't returning, I defined death as complete abandonment. I self-directed the anger and believed I had failed him and that is why he was not coming back. So facing death for me was crippling and overwhelming because it was all encompassing, characterized by fear, anger, and failure. The discomfort I felt with every death, every loss was paralyzing. My own therapy along with my clinical experience helped me deconstruct my fears, my vulnerability into manageable bites as I reconstructed my experiential knowledge defined by my life experiences. Fundamentally, I now believe that such feelings of discomfort while engaged in transformative learning prove as heuristic tools (Regan 2005; Giabiconi 2013), and I derive insight from them. Such experiential knowledge contributed to my sense of being.

For three years in the oncology and palliative care units,[4] I witnessed each individual's journey, interacted with many individual human beings and their experience of mortality and their lived realities. I was committed to be by their side, during their treatment, remission, or deathbed. Moreover, this choice of fieldwork exposed my vulnerability, my fears, and as a result, I was extremely uncomfortable with every referral, hoping each would end up in remission, and when they did not, I experienced a heightened discomfort and fear. It did not get easier, but it did become familiar. Nonetheless, with each patient I learned something new through each patient's personal narratives, respected their individual integrity, and consequently, I gained a better understanding and acceptance of my vulnerability and fears. Because time was of the essence, it challenged me to become a more empathic listener. On this one day, I had a referral from one of the oncologists for a patient in palliative care. On the referral, there was nothing more than "62-year-old male in palliative care, patient and family require psychological support stat." Every referral I received was marked urgent at my mental health clinic at the hospital. When I entered the room after completing my rounds in the palliative care unit, I noticed the room was empty and the scent of cancer was permeating the room. Cancer, the scent of the body decaying, has a distinct odor that I became accustomed to while working at the hospital, and it is a scent that to this day, I can still recognize. I said the patient's name again as I approached his bedside, and I noticed his body was not attached to any intravenous unit. The patient, John, had died, and his family had already left. It was just me and John in the room. I recall taking a deep breath and thinking here is my chance to face my fear, connect with my emotions, and not be focused on others in the room, just me and John, who for me was very much present. I felt a sense of loss as I did not get a chance to meet John before he died or meet his family, but I realized I met him in his death. It was not as bad as I expected it to be, no drama, just serenity and a sense of certainty, and at that moment this individual enabled my resolution, he granted me a sense of peace and acceptance with my mortality and mortality as a lived reality. I stayed there alone with John as long as I needed to. The significance of this clinical experience, as that with my indigenous patients, went beyond the boundaries of anthropology and psychology. It impacted me as I embraced my fear and vulnerability, and I felt more grounded in my identity, which in the end benefited my patients, their family members, my colleagues in their understanding of the patient's experience, as well as my university students with whom I shared such narratives.

SHARING MY EXPERIENCES IN THE FIELD

My experiences gain more meaning, are given an added dimension when I share them, as "storied conversations are an important part of our 'inner' life as well as playing a major role, perhaps *the* major role, in our 'outer,' public life" (Collins 2012, 240, author's emphasis). I open my self to experiences that are transformative and then open myself to sharing my experiences with my university students is as transformative. This translation comes with its own challenges, such as exposing my vulnerability, but in sharing my personal narratives I seek validation, and it enhances my sense of belongingness. As described in chapter 2, having been marginalized, this experience increases in relevance and resonance. Sharing my narratives of experience in the field becomes a critical part of my transformative process. As a professor, my main objective was to show that humanity is not incompatible with science or that passion is compatible with knowledge. And my message to my students was clear—it is important for anthropologists to 'get real' and to better understand relationships and to grasp "the pragmatism and imagination and feelings people reveal. . . . It is recognizing one's self, or another's as anything but given" (Battaglia 2000, 114–115). It is as critical to embrace the serendipitous and contingent dimension to fieldwork, ethnographic writing, learning and teaching, as it lends itself to storytelling.

With my students, I engaged in human-to-human interactions about storied memories of human-to-human interactions. The generation of narratives from my fieldwork to my students is a memory-creating experience (Collins

2010), and I would add, memory sustaining—the more I shared, the more I would remember details of my lived experiences. As Kohn (2010, 197) states,

> The memories become reworked due to the continually extended dialogic relationship the ethnographer has with her maturing self through her experiences with others. To recognize these subtle changes and allow for these altered framings to feature in our teaching and writing and 'knowing' is to revel in the *processes* of serendipity and reflexivity and to celebrate the often surprising nature of human interaction.

In my classes, whether it be cultural anthropology, psychological anthropology, medical anthropology, ethnography and fieldwork, race relations, Aboriginal studies, I engaged students in storied conversations, and I discovered that "telling stories of personal situations and feelings of discomfort permits to address larger anthropological debates, such as the academic/activist tension and ethical issues" (Giabiconi 2013, 199). Opening myself in the teaching milieu also conveyed the value I placed on the reflexivity involved in both the intra- and interdialogue that becomes evident in the teaching experience as well. The teaching became an extension to my research as well as an enabler to my self-transformation. Reflexivity is "a sensitizing notion that can enable ethical practice to occur in the complexity and richness of social research" (Guillemin and Gillam 2004, 278). Although I am not teaching classes as I used to, I remain on faculty as an adjunct professor, and so I supervise graduate students, and in my government position, I work closely with the university students who work in the department. I regularly hold sessions and share my stories from the field, my past and current challenges, and I always encourage them to reflect, and to not suppress but to value their subjectivity. Sharing my personal narratives with my students also becomes a moral practice, part of my ethical responsibility as an advocate and an important aspect of my role in the decolonization process and reconciliation.

NOTES

1. I am sure many policy analysts may feel that this is a bit of a stretch, but my view is that if the policies being developed affect people in communities, then reflection and developing an understanding of people, the community or communities should be a prerequisite in the initial phase of policy development.

2. I have to share that I am quite comfortable with the ambiguity inherent in just "being there," and this is definitely conducive to discovering serendipitous, unsought findings.

3. The maggots remained in her chest cavity to treat the infection. I had never heard about maggot therapy, and after discussing it with Pauline's infectious disease specialist and microbiologist, I learned how the secretions from maggots complement the part of the immune system that reacts to invading pathogens, which is crucial to clearing infections (cf. Arnold 2013).

4. When I started my government position, I unfortunately had to make the decision to end my clinical work given that my position entailed travelling to regions, and so I did not have the time to commit to both.

Chapter Six

Engaging in Reconciliation

Reconciliation starts with the individual, and so my personal engagement entails deconstructing and defining the tenets of my cultural lens. I need to self-reflect and define my own cultural biases so that they do not interfere with my understanding of cultures different from my own. Anthropology has greatly contributed to the critical insight that we cannot escape our own cultural biases because they form our lens and so we need to be aware of them and monitor that they do not lead to creating false assumptions of others who identify with cultures that differ from our own. I strongly believe that if we create false cultural assumptions, we feed stereotypes, and perhaps unintentionally breed colonialism. Thus, in order to engage in reconciliation, the first step is to identify one's lens, be reflexive, be open-minded, and listen empathically. The one patient I keep close in my memory as she inspires my engagement in reconciliation is Mary, whom I introduced in chapter 1 and who is a residential school survivor, whose tongue was cut by her school teacher because she refused to stop speaking her Cree mother tongue. Her persistence, bravery, and resilience even after such a traumatic experience continue to inspire me, while feeding my drive to learn from the past to not repeat the mistakes made by policy makers, and create a path of healthy and peaceful coexistence, where human rights and cultural diversity are respected and we learn from each other and together contribute to the growth of this nation. In this chapter, I will attempt to demystify reconciliation and describe its building blocks and show how building one's cultural competence plays a critical role. I will also outline the Indigenous Community Development government-wide training that I am currently engaged in (First Nations and Inuit Health Branch 2013), and I will show how this training is an important part of my efforts in reconciliation. We have so much to learn from our First Peoples, and we need to confront the reality of their experience of colonialism and heal with them rather than from the sidelines that separate us from their reality, which in essence is very much ours as well. "Too often, researchers have heard these stories without listening, listened without acting, acted without listening again. It is time to break that cycle" (Kelm 1998, xxiii).

Reconciliation is not an indigenous experience alone as we all have critical roles as allies in this process. "We cannot leave this critical task up to governments and the courts. In reality, institutions do not lead social change. The people do. And so it is up to us" (Regan 2005, 10). Although reconciliation needs to be part of our national agenda, breaking the cycle starts and rests with the individual. We each have a choice, indigenous and nonindigenous, to engage in critical inquiry, reflection, healing, social action, and change. Reconciliation requires personal commitment and a respect for the other—without these foundational elements, any effort is futile. My vision of North American-indigenous reconciliation is one that stresses affective awareness and interpersonal understanding, anchored in a widespread nonindigenous awareness of indigenous histories and aspirations (James 2012).

As illustrated in chapter 5, reflexivity requires using critical discursive practices of learning and synthesizing new information, including different worldviews and paradigms from our own. Reflexivity is not simply about learning about the other but understanding the perspective from which a person sees the world and both parties engaging subjectively in that process (Lennon 1995). Becoming a partner within the reconciliation process involves this type of reflexivity as well as empathy. Reconciliation involves learning from each other, integrating the knowledge into one's being, and constantly evolving, reflecting, and not remaining static (Laughton 2012). Before transcending "the old colonial roles and imperial mindsets that keep us trapped in a relationship defined by the historical dichotomies of oppressor/oppressed and perpetrator/victim," we need to understand our history of colonialism and cultural oppression (Regan 2005, 5). Broadening our knowledge about our history and current realities is the first building block of reconciliation. Cultural competence requires accurate knowledge of the history between nonindigenous and indigenous peoples.

BREAKING THE CYCLE—MOVING BEYOND THE "POST-COLONIAL DOOR"[1]

I was at a courthouse once representing four children, all siblings who had experienced significant neglect and abuse while living with their mother, who had issues with substance abuse. I was approached by a distant relative of mine who happened to be a detective in the police force. He asked why I was there, so I explained; and then he responded with a frown and in a loud inquisitive tone, "You work with savages?" As my heart was sinking to my feet, my anger and passion immediately lifted it and I responded, "Firstly, they are NOT savages, they are humans like you and me and maybe you should come to work with me in a First Nation community to see with your own eyes how they are far from being *savages*." Of course, there were many other selected words I would have liked to say at that point because I was outraged, but I left it at that. He nodded in disbelief and left. Daily, I hear from some family members, friends, and colleagues, all nonindigenous and who tend to be more ethnocentric, "Why do you bother with such a lost cause? Why are we taxpayers plugging money into such a black hole? Why bother with having a Department of Aboriginal Affairs if there is no progress in communities? Can Aboriginal people just get over it and move forward like others have? Why don't they just leave the reserves if they are not happy there?" These questions stem from ignorance and to me are indicative of how our society has nurtured such ignorance through our education system and propaganda. Ignorance is filled with cultural assumptions and myths about Aboriginal people. Also related to this ignorance is an anti-historical stance that such cultural oppression could have occurred and its effects continue to be present in our own backyard, that current living conditions in communities cannot be similar to Third World countries because we live in a First World country—but the reality is they are, I saw it with my own eyes. The ways that our education system, our propaganda feed these cultural assumptions and stereotypes from one generation to the next, breed intergenerational colonialism. I believe the only way to counter this and address the nonindigenous or settler complacency (Regan 2005, 2010) and ethnocentrism is through education and awareness-raising, and dialogue between indigenous and nonindigenous people. I have also witnessed in many of the individuals who have asked similar questions to those listed above a reparation displacement, which James (2009) describes as a resistance to repair injustice by denying responsibility or claiming no injustice has occurred and redirects responsibility on the victims alone, where the state and especially nonindigenous peoples are distanced from any accountability. I have also noticed in the few individuals who refuse to shake their complacency that such resistance tends to breed reparation displacement. Coexistence without empathy is both superficial and fragile, and so, authentic reconciliation requires an empathic recognition, a rehumanization of the other, and a rebuilding of individual relationships, which can lead to social reconstruction (Halpern and Weinstein 2004). As colonization was based on dehumanization, reconciliation has to be founded in empathic rehumanization. Without empathy, attempts at reconciliation are futile.

LISTENING TO THE SURVIVORS

In many of my encounters and especially my teachings that are driven by the objective to demystify and educate, many nonindigenous individuals have been able to address their antihistorical stance, shake their complacency, and better understand their reparation displacement, and as a result, they understand their role in reconciliation. Most often these individuals are usually shocked, angry, and disgusted with the truths of our history of human rights violation. Like one expressed to me, "Interesting how we don't have to go as far as Rwanda to see such cultural genocide and trauma—it happened right here in our own backyard!" I also encourage people to attend the Truth and Reconciliation Commission (TRC) events held across the country to hear directly from residential school survivors and their experiences of colonialism.[2] Listening to the oral testimonies of the survivors allows many to experience that empathic connection. The TRC is the most significant and direct attempt to promote reconciliation, inspired by the principles of restorative justice[3] (Sheppard 2013), and it took office immediately after the apology from the Canadian federal government to residential school survivors in 2008.[4] The Commission's overarching mission is to tell Canadians about the history of residential schools and the impact those schools have had on Aboriginal peoples, and to guide a process of national reconciliation (TRC 2012). For many survivors, the TRC is about truth finding as they feel that many Canadians remain in disbelief that such violations of human rights occurred in this country. In the words of a Métis Elder, "My mission is for others to hear about my life in the school, how I was severely abused but to also see my resilience. The message that we survived is also really important for people to hear." The TRC holds many national events during the year in various cities in Canada where residential school survivors have an opportunity to openly share what they had experienced, for them to connect with others through shared memories, establish bonds between generations, and to gain validation from others, especially nonindigenous peoples who come to listen and learn. There is also a National Film Board film (*We Were Children* 2012), *We Were Children*, where two survivors openly speak about their experiences in two separate residential schools. When I recently viewed this film for students and colleagues in my department, they were in a state of shock, and many were quite angry that such human rights' violations occurred in Canada and that this was in our recent past.[5] I and many others have realized that for most of the last century, the residential school story was perhaps the least-known dimension of Canadian history (TRC 2012). Listening to indigenous peoples' voices and their narrative re-enactment, whether they had positive or negative experiences as residential school survivors, is central to our engagement in reconciliation. Our engagement demands ethical listening, and necessitates follow-up discourses and activities in order to produce social change (Czyzewski 2011, 6). As Wilson (2003, 380) contends, anthropologists are uniquely positioned to instruct those attempting reconciliation in the practice of listening to help re-establish networks of trust among indigenous and nonindigenous peoples.

BALANCING THE HISTORICAL NARRATIVE

Pursuing reconciliation means sharing with and educating others not only about their experiences of injustices but also about their successes. Despite colonialism, their customs, their cultural diversity, their languages that were present before the settlers arrived have survived the effects of colonialism. We need to recognize that there is much more to indigenous history and lived realities than colonialism alone. It has definitely had a large impact on communities, and we all need to fully understand its implications, but what I would like to highlight is that indigenous communities had sustainable governance structures, as well as land and resource management regimes in place and they were well connected to their cultural ways and languages before their experience of cultural oppression and colonization. Colonization disrupted the stability of communities and their role in wider society (Alfred 2005). Before the European settlers arrived, Aboriginal peoples were self-governing societies, and this part of our history is also rarely told. Recognizing this historical existence of self-government, of sustainable communities is crucial in moving forward on the path of reconciliation because, in my opinion, it helps explain the resilience of the indigenous people and how they survived colonialism, with many of the cultures and languages in vibrant form today.

There are many historical accounts that show how indigenous and European settlers actually lived for many years in a peaceful, cooperative co-existence (Morantz 2002), working together, and learning from each other. To illustrate further, during the eighteenth and nineteenth century the fur-trading relationship between the Crees of Quebec and Ontario and the Hudson's Bay Company had been mutually beneficial. The greatest challenge to the Cree way of life came in the twentieth century, with the imposition of administration from the south and consequently the Crees had to confront a new group of foreigners whose ideas and plans were very different from those of the fur traders. In the 1930s and 1940s, government intervention helped overcome the disastrous disappearance of the beaver through the creation of government-decreed preserves and a ban on beaver hunting, but beginning in the 1950s a revolving array of socio-economic programs instituted by the government brought the adverse effects of what Morantz (2002) calls *bureaucratic colonialism*. Morantz draws on oral testimonies from Cree Elders and shows how their strong ties to the land and their appreciation of the wisdom of their way of life, coupled with the ineptness and excessive frugality of the Canadian bureaucracy, allowed them to escape the worst effects of colonialism. Despite becoming increasingly politically and economically dominated by Canadian society, the Crees succeeded in staving off cultural oppression. The nine Cree communities in Quebec came together as a nation and were able to face the massive hydroelectric development of the 1970s with their language, practices, and values intact and succeeded in negotiating the first modern treaty (Morantz 2002).

According to Matthew Coon Come, the Grand Chief of the Cree of Eeyou Istchee, the Quebec Region, "For the Crees, the *Indian Act* doesn't apply. We've changed the governance regime so we can be able to be involved in the way development takes place. . . . The Cree survived because we adapted" (CBC News 2013). When I share the Cree experience to the ethnocentric 'settlers,' I often get asked, "So why haven't other Aboriginal communities adapted?" There are varied reasons, and most often it has to do with communities being in crisis and thus do not have the infrastructure, such as leadership and capacity, in place to move forward. Such communities as I have mentioned are still experiencing intergenerational trauma[6] as a result of colonialism. "Historical social policies have impacted multiple generations of Aboriginal peoples. The severing of family and community has left a legacy of traumatized individuals who may be unable to function in mainstream society" (Menzies 2010, 69–70). For these communities, it will take more time to heal, reconnect with, and revitalize their cultural ways in order to have that strong base to adapt to change and continue to thrive. Healing from colonization and residential schools is the precursor to successful communities and community development (First Nations and Inuit Health Branch 2013). Healing from historic trauma varies from individuals and communities—as the trauma varied, the healing varies. Healing and decolonization do not occur in a linear fashion (Archibald 2006). Every individual and every community is different, albeit there are similarities. I do agree with Menzies' argument that it can be helpful for an indigenous patient to see the issues confronting them through a public policy lens so that it gives them "a sense that it was not issues of personal or genetic factors that contributed to their situation, but an array of public policies that shaped and defined their lives" (2010, 80).

ABORIGINAL RIGHTS IN CANADA

Many people I have met, especially those who have confronted me with the questions outlined above, have demonstrated a lack of understanding of Aboriginal rights. They are almost always surprised to hear that Aboriginal rights are founded on the historical reality that Aboriginal peoples lived in Canada prior to European occupancy. "Both history and the law of the land provide for differential treatment of several classes of people. Canadians should just learn to deal with the fact that Aboriginal peoples enjoy such rights" (White, Maxim, and Beavon 2004, 40). We all need to recognize that Aboriginal peoples have always been and will continue to be active and valuable contributors to the unfolding of our history. In 1982, the only amendment made to the Canadian Constitution was the inclusion of Section 35 relating to Aboriginal and treaty rights where the rights for First Nations, Métis, and Inuit in Canada were recognized and affirmed.[7] Section 35 is the part of the Constitution Act that recognizes and affirms Aboriginal rights. The Canadian government did not initially plan to include Aboriginal rights so extensively within the constitution when the Act was being redrafted in the early 1980s. Early drafts and discussions during the patriation of the Canadian Constitution did not include any recognition of those existing rights and relationships, but through campaigns and demonstrations, Aboriginal groups in Canada successfully fought to have their rights enshrined and protected. It is important to understand that Section 35 recognizes Aboriginal rights, but did not create or define them—Aboriginal rights have existed before Section 35. What Aboriginal rights include has been the topic of much debate and discussion, and they have been defined over time through several Supreme Court of Canada cases. Aboriginal rights have been interpreted to include a range of cultural, social, political, and economic rights including the right to land, as well as to fish, hunt, practice one's own culture, and to establish treaties (Asch 1984; McCabe 2010).

Although many First Nations feel that the promise of Section 35 is the antithesis to Indian Act regime that remains in place, which they feel promotes passivity and hinders progress, others, like the Crees in Quebec and many other First Nations, continue to forge ahead with the right to self-determination, as they define sovereignty in culturally appropriate terms. The Supreme Court of Canada has stated that the fundamental objective of Section 35 is reconciliation, which requires the government of Canada to balance the rights of Aboriginal people with those of non-Aboriginal Canadians. The most recent, landmark Supreme Court of Canada decision in the case of *Tsilhqot'in Nation v. British Columbia*, June 26, 2014, it clearly states that the government must further the goal of reconciliation with regard to both the Aboriginal interest and that of the broader public objective (*Tsilhqot'in Nation v. British Columbia* 2014, para 82). This decision has significant implications on curent comprehensive land claims or modern treaties' negotiations as Aboriginal groups may prefer to claim title through the court system rather than through the treaty negotiation process. Overall, this decision is being viewed as a game changer because it empowered Aboriginal people to push the government and industry to think more deeply about the meaning of reconciliation and how to work more effectively with Aboriginal partners in a more inclusive manner.

In the early 1990s, the Commission of Inquiry's mandate was to investigate the evolution of the relationship among Aboriginal people, the Canadian government and Canadian society as a whole, and after four years of extensive consultations and research, in 1996, the Royal Commission on Aboriginal Peoples (RCAP) released its final report. Being a member of the Native Mental Health Research unit at that time, I had contributed as a researcher in this whole process. The five-volume, four-thousand-page report covered a vast range of issues with its 440 recommendations that called for sweeping changes to the relationship between Aboriginal and non-Aboriginal people and governments in Canada. The RCAP set out an approach to self-government built on the recognition of Aboriginal governments as one of three orders of government in Canada. One of its major recommendations was that all governments in Canada—federal, provincial/territorial—recognize that the sphere of the inherent right of Aboriginal self-government encompasses core areas of jurisdiction, which include all matters that are of vital concern for the life and welfare of a particular Aboriginal people, as well as, peripheral areas of jurisdiction, which include all matters that have an impact on adjacent federal or provincial/territorial jurisdictions (RCAP 2011). An important overriding conclusion of the RCAP was the emphasis on restructuring, rebuilding, and renewing the relationship between indigenous and nonindigenous peoples. "The cooperative relationships that generally characterized the first contact between Aboriginal and non-Aboriginal people must be restored, and we believe that understanding just how, when and why things started to go wrong will help achieve this goal" (RCAP 2011). The relationship needs to be restructured fundamentally and grounded in ethical principles that everyone needs to apply and abide by. The RCAP led to various community-based healing programs, such as those funded through the Aboriginal Healing Foundation, which supported my art therapy program in communities for many years. The Aboriginal Healing Foundation is an Aboriginal-managed, national, nonprofit private corporation established in 1998, when the federal government provided a one-time grant as part of RCAP's *Gathering Strength: Canada's Aboriginal Action Plan*. The mandate was to encourage and support, through research and funding contributions, community-based, Aboriginal-directed healing initiatives that address the legacy of physical and sexual abuse suffered in Canada's residential school system, that led to intergenerational impacts (AHF 2013). Their mission is to help Aboriginal people heal themselves.

The RCAP was by far the most comprehensive effort to define a plan of reconciliation between the Aboriginal peoples of this land and the rest of Canadian society. When thinking about reconciliation in the current context, there are many reasons to turn to the RCAP as I see it as an important informative resource. The objectives of the residential school system were based on the false assumption that Aboriginal cultures and spiritual beliefs were inferior and unequal to the mainstream society and incapable of governing themselves. RCAP identified several other false assumptions in addition to what motivated and sustained the residential schools (Serson 2012). We need to ask whether there are other false assumptions motivating government policy on Aboriginal peoples, and if there are, we need to deconstruct them so they do not confound efforts to achieve reconciliation. I think it is critical to keep the RCAP in the foreground of policy development because its recommendations remain relevant today, even after eighteen years. It is a great resource to support the process of deconstructing colonial policies that promote detrimental discursive environments (Czyzewski 2011). Since RCAP, we have seen intensive and increasing efforts at healing and recovery in communities, community development, and many community-driven processes whether in the form of education, self-government, or socioeconomic development. Healing and community development can take time, and government efforts to support such processes can be incremental, but we have seen progress since RCAP, and I believe there is more to follow. A critical cultural and paradigm shift needs to occur in our society and especially at the level of government to best support decolonization, rehumanization, and reconciliation. As Regan (2010, 237) so eloquently writes, "reconciliation is . . . a teaching/learning place of encounter where acts of resistance and freedom occur. This involves nothing less than a paradigm shift that moves us from a culture of denial toward an ethics of recognition." What would greatly support this cultural and paradigm shift is an insurgent education movement (Corntassel and Holder 2008), which I believe the Indigenous Community Development training that I will describe next is becoming.

INDIGENOUS COMMUNITY DEVELOPMENT TRAINING[8]

The past is in front of us and the future is behind us. We know what happened, we can see our past, it lies in front of us, but we don't know what the future holds and so that's why it is behind us. We can look before us and learn from the past so we have a better future.—Elder Woody Morrison Jr., Indigenous Community Development Training Session, Vancouver, June 2013

Within the past four years in my government position, I have been collaborating with colleagues in the First Nations and Inuit Health Branch of Health Canada in developing the curriculum for the Indigenous Community Development, two-day training for bureaucrats. This training represents my contribution to moving reconciliation beyond abstraction to concrete action. The training is founded on developing one's cultural competence in hopes to not repeat the mistakes of the past and to learn how to best support community development and capacity building. It focuses on the building blocks of cultural competence, and its definition is based on the framework applied by the New Zealand *Wharerata* (pronounced as *fare eh rata*) Declaration, the Canadian cultural competence standard for physicians, as well as the First Nations Health Managers Association framework. Cultural competence is a lifelong journey that starts with the accurate knowledge of our country's history and current realities, specifically the history of Canada's relationship with Aboriginal people; builds on self-awareness, which requires personal intent; and it leads to building effective relationships and networks of trust.

For the two-day training session, we have an Elder with us, and he or she is actively involved in the whole process, providing guidance and support to the trainers and the trainees. We engage in a truth-telling dialogue where an Elder shares his or her experience of oppression as well as resilience, which helps participants deconstruct the myths of our national history of indigenous-settler relations. This training creates a space that ultimately transforms the nonindigenous participant and empowers the indigenous Elder. We educate about the impact of colonization as well as highlight the strength of the human spirit and profound sacredness of human dignity. Regan (2010, 53) describes the dialogue circle methodology she uses in her workshop, *Unsettling Dialogues of History and Hope*, as being based on dialogue that addresses "power imbalances, cultural differences, and traumatic histories, thus providing safe space for emotional expression." Similarly, in part of the Indigenous Community Development training session, the dialogue circle methodology is also applied to create a safe place where participants feel recognized and in turn, empowered.[9] We also have a mental health professional, like me, who is present for participants who may need emotional support during the training. The Elder, the mental health professional, and the team of dedicated and trained facilitators help foster a culturally safe environment for the training session. This training encourages participants to engage in critical inquiry. Like Regan, the pedagogy of discomfort or transformative learning offers participants an opportunity to rethink our collective history, re-educate themselves in hopes that they sustain their rethinking and engage in the decolonization process.

The Community Development Framework and its associated Indigenous Community Development training were adopted in 2012 by the two federal departments in Canada that focus primarily on supporting Aboriginal communities—that is, Health Canada and Aboriginal Affairs and Northern Development Canada. The Community Development Framework (Figure 6.1) is based on an extensive research and interviews with many Aboriginal community leaders and academics. This image is the logo for the Indigenous Community Development training, and it was designed by a First Nation artist. It represents the longhouse, the igloo, and the teepee to reflect and respect First Nations and Inuit cultural relevance and diversity.

Three pillars on the outside are the entry points—that is, community capacity, knowledge and competencies of partners, and partnerships for community well-being; and the five principles appear in the inside circle—indigenous knowledge and culture, strength based, community centred, community leadership, and holistic well-being. The Framework is centred in cultural competence. The Framework and training are also supported by the National Aboriginal Organizations in Canada, namely, the Assembly of First Nations and the Inuit Tapiriit Kanatami. The training is currently optional, and it is gaining momentum because its objective is resonating with government workers and indigenous peoples alike. To date, we have had over 1,200 participants, and we have brought this training to various regions in the Canada. The objective of the training is to embed community development knowledge and expertise within policy development processes, so that policy analysts and senior managers across departments apply their cultural competence and translate their knowledge into policies and programs that will as a result be more culturally relevant and locally meaningful. A critical component of the cultural competence toolkit is the knowledge base, and in addition to sharing knowledge and enlightening participants with the history of indigenous-settler relations, we also emphasize the need for bureaucrats to be trauma-informed. The curriculum addresses trauma and intergenerational trauma, and the reason this is such a critical aspect of cultural competence is

Figure 6.1.   The Community Development Framework (First Nations and Inuit Health Branch 2013)

because it is the current lived reality of many indigenous communities. And so if we are to support culturally based healing and community-driven initiatives, then we should be aware of what the people in the community are experiencing as a result of past injustices caused by government policies. As a First Nation participant said in one of our sessions, "It is about time we do something like this. Our people need to see that there are public servants who care to learn about our past and our current reality." We also highlight the federal government's recent, tangible gesture of reconciliation, which commemorates the legacy of Indian Residential Schools through a permanent installation of stained glass artwork in a window of the Centre Block on Parliament Hill (Figure 6.2). It was installed in Parliament on the four-year anniversary of the Apology to the Survivors of Residential Schools from the Prime Minister, Stephen Harper.[10] This window encourages Parliamentarians, as well as visitors to Parliament for generations to come, to learn about the history of Indian Residential Schools and Canada's reconciliation efforts (A. A. Canada 2013). Designed by the Métis artist, Christi Belcourt, this intricate, storytelling, stained glass window is entitled *Remembering the Past: A Window to the Future-'Giniigaaniimenaaning.'* *Giniigaaniimenaaning* means 'looking ahead' in Ojibwe, with an emphasis that *everyone* is looking ahead toward the future for the ones who are yet unborn. The story starts in the bottom left, pre-contact period where cultural ways were intact, moving up through the story of colonization and cultural genocide, and then around towards the rights through the story of cultural revitalization. Essentially, in the training we highlight the symbolism of this window, first as a symbolic gesture by the federal government and second, as one that speaks to reconciliation as mutual sharing, learning about our collective past, and relationship building. Although the process of reconciliation remains ongoing, there is still remains much more to learn, support, and contribute. The window is the most explicit and symbolic demonstration of the government's commitment to reconciliation (cf. Dwyer 2003).

Community development is a principled, values-based approach to support better outcomes in First Nations, Inuit, and Métis well-being. Because community development happens from within, government cannot actually "do" community development. The foundational value and belief of community development is that the people themselves can improve their community by working together, building consensus on priorities and actions, building on community assets including culture, and developing individual and community capacity. Indigenous community development is dependent on the combined capacities of the community's individuals, its leadership and governance, and the public service. The role of governments and partners is to support the capacity of community, individuals, organizations, and governance excellence. For governments and partners, strengthened knowledge and competencies (including cultural competence) in effectively part-

Figure 6.2. Stained Glass Window Commemorating the Legacy of Indian Residential Schools in the Parliament building

nering with communities, and strengthened community partnerships are necessary elements for success. Therefore, it becomes very important for
government workers to have an accurate knowledge of how 1) to support
community developers, 2) to support their capacity, 3) to build effective
relationships with the community developers to best support them, and 4) to
build effective relationships between federal departments to help reduce
some of the barriers that communities face.

In another part of the training, we address the components of a community development continuum, which is also based on extensive research as
well as ethnographic interviews with community leaders. As mentioned earlier, prior to contact and colonization, communities were stable and successful. Some communities continue to struggle with the impacts of colonization.
The four quadrants of the community development continuum include: paralysis or crisis, coping, rebuilding, and successful collaborating. There are in
reality very few communities at any given time that are in a serious state of
crisis, and I have visited a couple of them wherein some lateral violence[11]
and substance abuse prevailed and in a few others, there was a suicide every
four to six weeks. In these communities, the common denominator was the
loss of cultural identification and a state of learned helplessness. The communities in crisis are fragmented with formal and informal leaders (i.e.,
Elders and youth) not ready to come together and the healing process yet to
begin. The significant difference between crisis and the coping stage is that
adults in these communities are starting to heal. One rarely sees a community
in crisis hold a community meeting, as the trust is not there. A community in
the coping stage can hold a gathering, but there is still internal conflict. The
shift from coping to rebuilding is more of a progression, and it is here that
capacity development is fundamental as it supports the progression. Communities that are rebuilding are those that are beginning to work together and
plan over multiple years, as seen in communities who have developed their
community plans. Most First Nation, Inuit, and Métis communities in Canada are in this rebuilding phase. A key point in this stage is that the community starts to define its own vision for the future, apart from what government
funders demand. The youth, women, and Elders have a voice and experience
a sense of place in community. In the rebuilding stage, a community proves
to itself that it can actually engage in what is needed and be successful. It is
particularly important for youth to witness this progression. As described in
chapter 4, in the Roots and Shoots Aboriginal Youth projects, youth leaders
have emerged in communities that are rebuilding due to empowered community members who are engaged in the healing process, and participating
actively in community gatherings. I have seen communities regress from
rebuilding back to a crisis phase when a suicide occurred. However, because
they have the experience of coming together as a community, they tend to
apply their assets and come together as a community to heal from the crisis.

In many communities I worked in as a clinician and visited as a bureaucrat, the progress from rebuilding to success is characterized by a sense of confidence and belongingness, where members learn from their Elders so they sustain their connection to their culture, language, and community. The shift from rebuilding to success, communities tend to rebuild the connections to and build partnerships with neighbors, communities that are both Aboriginal and non-Aboriginal, as demonstrated by the T'Souke First Nation community discussed in chapter 4. The lesson for government in applying this community development continuum is to target supports based on where the communities may be and what they need. It is not to slot communities in a fixed stage but to better understand where they are at and how government can best support the shift from one phase to the next.

Community development is built on individual and organizational capacities, which are the building blocks for community development. Governments should not compromise community capacity, decision-making, self-determination, and hope. The more directive government is, the more that undermines communities' capacity, as directive programs and policies attenuate the community's decision-making capacity and initiative. Governments should focus on opportunities for communities to leverage partnerships to support capacity development in individuals and organizations. I believe that if government wants to see positive outcomes, then we need to be responsive to Aboriginal peoples, and investments should focus on long-term, sustainable capacity development that is community based, community paced, and community led. The more the community experiences a sense of ownership over its own development, the more it is sustained. What is also required is to break down silos at the government level, collaborate more within each federal department, collaborate between departments and provincial /territorial governments, and work with innovative partners—such as corporations and nonprofits to support community well-being—as the community requests. The more we network, the more we decrease the risk of unintended consequences.[12] As Coon Come also contends, "You need to allow the First Nations to participate, to be participants in the development of the territory, [whether] it be forestry, mining, or any other industry that may come" (CBC News 2013). Indigenous people need to be active participants in policy development related to their well-being and their community and not passive recipients of policies that are detached from their local realities. In partnership, government and communities need to ensure we do not replicate the harms of the past.

WALKING THE TALK

My personal engagement in reconciliation is multifaceted. It is founded on my belief that indigenous people of this nation deserve better—they deserve to be included in the fabric of our society and respected as integral contributors. Without indigenous peoples, we would not have a nation. My engagement is defined by my belief that reconciliation is a North American experience, not an indigenous one alone. Reconciliation *is* an ongoing relationship-building process (Blackburn 2007). There is no plan, no model on how to engage in decolonization or reconciliation (Barker 2010). All I know and have authority on is my action, my critical consciousness, my ethical commitment to address past injustices and restore human dignity. My role as ally also entails educating other Canadians about the indigenous-Canadian history, about current realities, and about the cultural diversity among indigenous groups. I strongly believe that knowledge translates into action, and so our understanding of the history, its impact, and how to be good partners has a huge impact on the quality of our relationship with communities. As bureaucrats, we have influence over our own competencies, and we continue to learn and build partnerships—we, as a result, increase our own effectiveness. Another facet of my engagement is to ensure we are developing policies that exemplify the principles of community development as described earlier, policies that are culturally relevant and that support sustainable community development. In terms of reconciliation, rather than distancing and mystifying it, it is important it becomes an experience-near process, to borrow Wikan's (2012) expression. Reconciliation is a loaded word, and often people and public servants alike fear it because it is made to be so intangible and therefore considered unattainable. The Indigenous Community Development training helps us bring reconciliation home. The training is a transformative approach to reconciliation that challenges prevailing settler or nonindigenous understanding, and it involves the settlers to engage in introspection (James 2012). A handful of colleagues see this training as an interesting aside, related to my previous clinical work and not completely relevant to our current policy work because as one said, "In our policy world, we are dealing with collectivities and not individuals." Such thinking promotes a disconnect between the individual and the collectivity, which is contrary to indigenous thinking where the two are interdependent. They simply do not understand that in communities that have experienced cultural oppression, healing, community development, and reconciliation may start with the individual, but it has a ripple effect and it becomes contagious, thus, affecting the collectivity or community. Despite the resistance or misconception by some, my Indigenous Community Development team and I forge ahead as in every training session evaluation, participants voice how this training is "filling a critical gap in our bureaucracy," "it is the missing link," and "it is helping me reconnect with my purpose as a public servant." The comments are from both indigenous and nonindigenous public servants. The training is becoming the catalyst for many to engage in the process of reconciliation.

Finally, my engagement is also founded on ground truthing and listening to the narratives of residential school survivors and of our Elders and validating their voices. It is so critical that in my interactions I do not sound deterministic, ethnocentric, and that I remain respectful of indigenous people as well as nonindigenous people because I realized that if you do not demonstrate empathy, you cannot expect to trigger it in others. In listening and gaining, sharing and translating knowledge, and interacting with others, authenticity remains key. My engagement in reconciliation, like my cultural competence, is *my* lifelong journey. As an Algonquin colleague told me with great enthusiasm, "You are walking the talk of a compassionate bureaucrat!"

NOTES

1. The term "post-colonial door" is derived from the British Columbia Assembly of First Nations, 2012 *Governance Toolkit—Guide to Community Engagement: Navigating Our Way Beyond the Post-Colonial Door*, which has been acclaimed as the most comprehensive report of its kind in Canada, setting out what First Nations in British Columbia are doing with respect to transitioning their governance from under the Indian Act to a postcolonial world based on recognition of Aboriginal title and rights (see www.bcafn.ca).

2. The Indian Residential School Settlement Agreement (IRSSA) is a comprehensive settlement package negotiated in 2007 between the Government of Canada, the churches, lawyers representing survivors, and the Assembly of First Nations. This package includes a cash payment for all former students of residential schools, healing funds, a truth and reconciliation commission, and commemoration funding (TRC 2012).

3. Restorative justice is grounded in the belief that those most affected by injustice should have the opportunity to become actively involved in the resolution of conflict. Direct engagement through dialogue is central to the practice of restorative justice (Umbreit et al. 2005). This social movement draws on the strengths of individuals and their capacity to openly address the need to heal through authentic humane engagement and responsibility taking and accountability, all conducive to reconciliation (Menkel-Meadow 2007, 180; Umbreit et al. 2005).

4. For the statement of the apology, see www.aadnc-aandc.gc.ca/eng/1100100015644.

5. The last residential school in Canada closed in 1996 (*We Were Children* 2012).

6. This term was developed by indigenous scholars (see Wesley-Esquimaux and Smolewski 2004).

7. Section 35 of the Constitution Act states: (1) The existing aboriginal and treaty rights of the aboriginal peoples of Canada are hereby recognized and affirmed. (2) In this Act, "Aboriginal peoples of Canada" includes the Indian, Inuit and Métis peoples of Canada. (3) For greater certainty, in subsection (1) "treaty rights" includes rights that now exist by way of land claims agreements or may be so acquired. (4) Notwithstanding any other provision of this Act, the aboriginal and treaty rights referred to in subsection (1) are guaranteed equally to male and female persons. (For more information see: http://laws-lois.justice.gc.ca/eng/const/page-16.html).

8. In the following section, the material is derived from the Indigenous Community Development Training (First Nations and Inuit Health Branch 2013).

9. Forget (2003) elaborates further on the application of "community circles," which is a restorative justice model to provide recognition and empowerment to all participants.

10. For the video of the *Indian Residential Schools Statement of Apology—Prime Minister Stephen Harper*, see: http://www.aadnc-aandc.gc.ca/eng/1100100015677/1100100015680.

11. Lateral violence occurs when community members strike out at each other as a result of being oppressed. The oppressed become the oppressors of themselves and each other. In many communities in crisis, I have witnessed such lateral violence, and it is most often due to individuals experiencing intergenerational trauma.

12. As Norton (2008) writes, "The law of unintended consequences, often cited but rarely defined, is that actions of people—and especially of government—always have effects that are unanticipated or unintended."

Chapter Seven

Ethical Responsibility

Anthropologists have been challenged recently to elaborate further on morality and ethical discourse, and the broad subdiscipline of anthropology of morality has emerged (Lambek 2010; Fassin 2012). As Fassin (2008) notes, anthropologists have been reluctant to enter this field of research, and I think it is mostly due to the fact that philosophers, anthropologists, and other theorists have made it into a complex rhetorical paradigm. Similar to the concept of reconciliation, social and political scientists have created an experience-distant,[1] intangible domain rather than an experience-near, tangible concept with practical resonance and coherence. It is not to say that ethics is not complex but that we should focus on how we each define it within our field of study and how we apply this in practice. To me, ethics is defined as commitment and personal integrity, and perhaps my definition is more similar to what Mattingly (2012) refers to as a "first-person" or "humanist" virtue ethics, yet it does resemble Foucauldian ethics with respect to the process of self-formation as an ethical subject (Foucault 1990, 29). In this chapter, I will deconstruct the domain of ethics and illustrate how my ethical approach is applied in practice in terms of creating an ethical space. As reconciliation starts with individual commitment, ethical responsibility starts with ethical self-awareness. "The professional ethic rests on the personal and draws its strength from it" (C. Geertz 1968, 157). For me, it draws from my integrity. I believe that in practicing my ethical responsibility in my daily affairs and especially in my work, I am expressing my integrity. What reverberates in my being is the echo of my grandfather's teachings: to practice integrity when no one is watching.

In chapter 6, I noted that the foundation of cultural competence is knowledge but interestingly, in Ben-Ari and Strier's (2010) reconceptualization of cultural competence using Emmanuel Levinas's theory, ethics precedes knowledge, which essentially means that the pursuit of knowledge is a secondary feature to the ethical duty toward the Other, and so I will elaborate further on this sense of obligation and how it relates to cultural competence. I will illustrate the code of ethics within government and anthropology, and the common fundamental element in practicing an ethical responsibility is authentic human-to-human interaction, authentic to self and other. I will also share how much I have learned from my indigenous partners and how my work ethic has been informed and enriched by these interactions. Regan (2010, 13) contends we need to "risk interacting differently with indigenous peoples—with vulnerability, humility," and I have to say that it was never a risk for me, as it always came naturally to interact in such a way. I also keep thinking of the artwork I created with Luke, my first ever Cree patient in art therapy, which was also my first encounter with an indigenous person, and how he was adamant about me drawing with him, which in essence was about me partnering with him in his healing process. It was a request that was spontaneous and authentic for Luke. And so, I mirrored the spontaneity and authenticity in agreeing to draw with him and respond to this initial step to building common ground. It was also the meeting of my vulnerability and his, where neither myself nor his was isolated. The only 'risk' I took was that of being judged by my supervisor, who would have preferred I maintain a detached, more stoic approach with respect to Luke's request to engage in the art-making process. So I feel I have come full circle, and the difference now is I have no hesitation of partnering and that I am pleased I followed my gut back then with Luke, and that I applied an experience-near, empathic approach to therapy rather than a detached one, as it elicited new discoveries and insights for both Luke and me.

"I AM BECAUSE YOU ARE."

My first responsibility has always been to those whose lives and cultures I encounter, study, learn from, and work with. I strongly feel that because the indigenous peoples I have worked with and those I continue to work with enrich my sense of self, I find myself accountable and responsible to respond to our relationships. This moral standard has always been an integral element of my core being, and although it has set me apart in the mainstream Western society, it has resonated with my indigenous partners, where individual identity is commonly defined through one's responsibility to others. This is similar to the ethical attitude espoused by the philosopher Emmanuel Levinas, who reminds us that the very possibility for subjectivity and individuality comes in the approach of the Other, and so our obligation is to respond to the relationship (Levinas 1998; Gehrke 2010; Ben-Ari and Strier 2010). A sense of responsibility is naturally assumed. When I engage with and listen to another individual, I am touched by their absolute dignity and their vulnerability (Ben-Ari and Strier 2010), and it is their vulnerability that requires me to connect with my ethical responsibility to create a safe place to allow for the individual to express themselves. Whether as a clinician or as a policy creator, I feel it is my responsibility to translate my awareness of the other's vulnerability into compassionate action by listening, validating, and learning from the other. Levinas's philosophy is similar to Michel Foucault's approach in terms of ethics being defined as the type of relationship one should have with oneself, *un rapport à soi* (Foucault 1984, 352). Both Foucault and Levinas claim that we as social scientists should not reduce the notion of self or the other, and both focus on how the self is constituted as an ethical subject; however, Levinas calls for a radical openness to the alterity of the Other, and how the relationship we have with another contributes to one's sense of self. Another distinction between both philosophical approaches is that Levinas, unlike Foucault, attends to one's articulation of ethics with other persons and how the relationship contributes to the constitution of the self as an ethical subject.[2] The process of self-formation as an ethical subject involves the monitoring, improving, and transforming oneself as Foucault (1990, 29) argues, but also influenced by and reflective of the relationship one has with others, as Levinas (1998) contends.

I consider Levinas's emphasis on another's subjective experience similar to the Ubuntu humanistic philosophy, which originated in South Africa, and the value of "*ubuntu*" translated refers to "I am because you are," which resonates with my experience and belief that one's sense of self is socially constructed. In practice, *ubuntu* refers to face-to-face understanding between two human beings (Halpern and Weinstein 2004, 565), emphasizing the link between the individual and the collective.[3] Shutte (2001) argues that Ubuntu philosophy complements rather than opposes the central Western notion of individual freedom and shows how the two notions can form an ethic based on a richer understanding of our humanity. In this chapter, I will further deconstruct the power dynamic present in Western-indigenous relations and apply Levinas's notion that the 'the Other' is *not* an object of the self, which is unlike Western traditional philosophy, and that our humanity evolves through the humanity of others (Ben-Ari and Strier 2010). This power dynamic continues to be present in Western-indigenous relations, and so in order for decolonization to occur, we need to create that ethical space where the dynamic is that the two human communities are on equal footing, engaged in face-to-face understanding.

I believe I, like all other North Americans and Canadians in particular, have benefited from the injustices made onto indigenous peoples, and thus, it is my ethical responsibility to perhaps not give back what was taken away simply because this is not possible, but to recognize our recent history and transform my guilt and outrage by nurturing my duty and passion to be a trustful ally, to effect change, and to engage in reconciliation. Although connecting with one's moral obligations while detaching from one's complacency may feel uncomfortable at times, this discomfort as I have experienced is more heuristic than paralysing (Fassin 2008, 342). Whether anthropologist, bureaucrat, or both, it is clear to me that we need to integrate an ethical responsibility toward the people we work with, and because we are working with and for other human beings, we cannot escape our moral obligations. Cultural competence and communicative competence entails an in-depth sense of ethical responsibility founded in respect for the other and oneself, and thus, it should center on the ethical nature of the relationship between the other and oneself. Gaining knowledge, being reflexive, and establishing relationships require intent, which is contingent on one's ethical responsibility. As an anthropologist, I agree I "must find a way to . . . integrate the quest for knowledge (of nature, of injustice and folly, and of self) with a ceaseless search for ways to apply this knowledge to the care of the self and of others" (Biehl, Good, and Kleinman, 2007, 32). Like reflexive awareness, ethical responsibility is a fundamental item in anthropology's moral agenda (D'Andrade 1995), and one cannot exist without the other. As Battaglia writes, ". . . any ethically aware social theory of contingency fulfills its potential insofar as it engages cultural difference in subjects' own terms, and undertakes its own ongoing self-analysis within sight of the dialogic, inherently contingent enterprise of ethnography" (2000, 115). As anthropologists, we have our own moral standards, and we need to learn the local moral standards through the establishment of relationships and our learning experiences in the field (Carrithers 2005) and through our own self-reflection.

MORAL ACTION WITHIN BUREAUCRACY

Bureaucratic expediency requires that identities are typified and made static, and so I feel responsible as an applied anthropologist working as a bureaucrat to ensure that the voices of individuals and communities are not silenced, and that policies developed are responsive to their lived realities. We as policy creators often get caught in the web that bureaucratic expediency creates, and so we need to stop, pull back, and think about the people being directly affected by the policies we develop. We as policy creators are not static, and thus why should we develop policies that force individuals and collectives into such static categories? As bureaucrats it is our responsibility to connect the dots, navigate the system, reduce barriers, and create networks to provide the best support possible for the people and communities we serve. I feel it my duty to contribute to the betterment of humanity as an advocate or public anthropologist working in the public sector (Scheper-Hughes 2009) and advancing reconciliation. As anthropologists, we should consider as one of our responsibilities "the task of furthering public accountability in complex societies" (Jorgensen 1971, 331).

Many of the elements I have addressed in previous chapters are all founded on being ethically responsible to those I work with and being responsible for and committed to taking a more proactive role in the process of decolonization. It is our collective responsibility to do what is necessary to ensure that indigenous people heal, develop, and contribute to the nation. As I presented in chapter 6, I feel it crucial to consider both my professional and personal role in the reconciliation process and the moral imperative to progress forward and undo colonial legacies. The Truth and Reconciliation Commission in Canada is about truth telling and truth finding by listening directly from the victims who were traumatized by the residential school legacy. It is also about Canadians confronting these past injustices and tapping into our personal and public moral values, leading to constructing a new, shared vision of the nation. As an anthropologist/advocate, I feel responsible to carry this truth through government where the decisions that are made affect the fates of people we study and care for (Mahmood 2002, 2). In adopting a position of advocacy, we need to ensure that the voices or experiences of the other are not appropriated (Kirmayer et al. 2011), and we need to grant primacy and validity to these personal narratives as they contribute to building our knowledge and, ultimately, our cultural competence as bureaucrats. We cannot resolve the injustices of the past, nor are we responsible for the decisions made in the past, but individually and together we are responsible for taking action today, for choosing to learn from the past, for acknowledging the injustices, and for choosing to become an active participant in the reconciliation process. Our cultural competence *is* an ethical requirement (Allen-Meares 2007) as it determines whether our work is successful in terms of building effective relationships and developing culturally relevant policies.

During the Indigenous Community Development training, I often highlight that we as public servants do have values and a code of ethics, and developing our cultural competencies is well aligned with our expected code of conduct (Treasury Board of Canada Secretariat 2011). We are expected to abide by this code and demonstrate the values of the public sector in our actions and behavior, such as respect for others; acting with integrity; demonstrating excellence by continuing to improve the quality of policies, programs, and services; and fostering a collaborative work unit. The federal departments and agencies are expected to integrate these values into their decisions, actions, policies, processes, and systems. We are expected to provide decision makers with all the information, analysis, and advice they need, always striving to be open, candid, and impartial. Treating all people with respect, dignity, and fairness is fundamental to our relationship with the public, and we should value diversity and the ideas the public generates as they are the source of our innovation. Integrity is considered the cornerstone of good governance, and engagement, collaboration, effective teamwork, and professional development are all essential to continually improving the quality of policies, programs, and services provided (Secretariat 2011). I think it is a critical reminder to link values to moral action because we usually get so busy in our daily affairs at work that we tend to unfortunately forget that this code is in place. It is not that we do not practice our values and ethics—it is more that we do not really connect with them. Developing our cultural competence helps us as public servants attach meaning to our values and ethics, and the more we apply them, the more they resonate. This code of ethics is quite similar to the code for anthropologists as outlined by the American Anthropological Association (2013), both founded on the moral position of the recognition of the worth of others. Carrithers (2005, 437) suggests that the recognition of others is necessarily entwined with the understanding of others, which lies at the heart of ethnographic research, and I would say the same for policy development, or at least it should be. The moral aesthetic is inevitably built into the condition of anthropological research as it entails the creation and understanding of social relations, and so I suggest that the development of policies that affect individuals in communities should be framed by the same moral aesthetic.

In anthropology, our ethnographic accounts reflect the worth of the anthropologist, the informants' worth, and the value of the relationships built during fieldwork. There is worth in our ethnographies as stories, worth of the ethnographer and the informants as storytellers. In the end, "anthropological knowledge amounts to a morality of mutual recognition, mutual trust, and mutual forbearance" (Heidegren 2005, 449). This morality of mutual recognition and trust and the integrity of our work need to be translated into the realm of policy development, which is done through engagement and relationship building with our partners and stakeholders. The more we engage, the more we learn, the better we network and more effectively broker knowledge, which in the end leads to the development of more responsive policies.

LEARNING FROM OUR ELDERS

As much as learning from Elders informs our cultural competence, it is as important in our connection to our ethical responsibility. Our professional code of ethics should be informed by Elders and the wisdom and knowledge that come from oral traditions. I think this knowledge and wisdom from Elders is applicable and relevant to professional codes of ethics across the public sector because of the value placed on relationships, respect, and integrity. We at Aboriginal Affairs and Northern Development Canada need to raise the value of indigenous knowledge and wisdom more so across the federal government family to show its potential to help guide policy analysts and decision makers with their daily challenges. As many of my colleagues from various government departments have expressed, indigenous knowledge and wisdom help ground them, making them better prepared, more confident to engage in strategic discussions and collaborative working relationships. I believe that as youth in communities need to connect with their Elders to reconnect with their cultural identity, we the nonindigenous settlers need to do the same to learn from, engage with, and appreciate their knowledge, their narratives that represent the richness of the varied indigenous cosmologies. In my life, Elders have always played a fundamental and influential role, from my grandparents to Elders I have had the honor and pleasure to meet with, learn from, and build relationships with. In the office building of the federal department where I work—that is, Aboriginal Affairs and Northern Development of Canada—there is a lodge called "the Kumik," and it offers a unique experience for employees to enter into an environment where they can stimulate a greater understanding and appreciation of Aboriginal cultures, philosophies, and practices. The Kumik predominantly provides employees with instruction and counsel through interaction with with Elders[4] who visit the lodge. The Kumik hosts Elders from First Nation, Inuit, and Métis communities across North America. Elders share personal narratives and their knowledge, beliefs, spirituality, and traditional customs. They conduct traditional spiritual ceremonies as requested for meetings and conferences, and they advise on how these cultural rituals can be rendered compatible with requirements of the contemporary workplace. The Kumik provides employees the opportunity to further develop our cultural competencies and continue to build on our awareness of cultural differences and similarities. Through the dynamic interactions with the Elders, employees can learn and appreciate differences in attitude, values, and assumptions, which oftentimes lead to more effective group and/or interpersonal communications. In sum, by listening to the teachings, employees can apply practical knowledge to how they communicate with others. Employees can also benefit from private sessions with Elders. The Kumik provides the space for Aboriginal and non-Aboriginal peoples working together to learn more about each other's realities (Neveu 2010).

Although the Kumik is located in a government building, it is not simply another boardroom. When one enters the lodge, one is surrounded by cedar walls and many meaningful cultural symbols that are placed throughout the room, such as sweet grass, tobacco, drums, eagle feathers, and beaded items. Visitors to the lodge are given the opportunity to smudge at the beginning of each teaching, which is a traditional cleansing practice that involves the burning of sacred medicines, such as sage, sweet grass, and cedar. The presence of the Elders and the ambience create a space, one of retreat and spiritual rejuvenation. Elders share their wisdom through storytelling, healing circles, teachings, and open discussions, and they provide the opportunity for visitors to participate in traditional activities, such as beading wampum belts or creating birch bark baskets. The Kumik plays a prominent role in training students in Aboriginal community awareness. For policy creators, having access to the Elders in the Kumik can allow them to be reminded of the priorities of the communities where the policies will be implemented. The Kumik definitely facilitates improvement of the quality of service we provide to the Aboriginal clientele. The rotation of Elders at the Kumik allows employees to experience the spiritual practices of various Nations and receive feedback on their questions from varying points of view. It is beneficial for employees to communicate with Elders on an ongoing basis in order to have an informed approach of the Aboriginal communities they serve and to create more effective and culturally relevant policies.

The Kumik was influential in promoting Aboriginal leadership in federal government especially through the development of the Aboriginal Leadership Development Initiative. Elders play a critical role in advising, transferring knowledge and beliefs to support the next generation of leaders. This initiative supports the department of Aboriginal Affairs and Northern Development Canada's goal of talent management, succession planning, and innovative learning, as well as support employees' well-being. This initiative also collaborates with the Committee for the Advancement of Native Employment, which explores and recommends ways to increase the number of Aboriginal employees in the department, and to retain them. The Kumik greatly influenced the cultural enrichment characteristic of this initiative, which supports Aboriginal employees' careers and nurtures their well-being and cultural identities.

Learning from indigenous Elders' teachings about relationships with others, the land, language, and ceremonies is extremely powerful, and it is a decolonizing imperative (Alfred and Corntassel 2005). I believe that the Kumik represents a great opportunity for policy analysts to tap into this grassroots level and integrate this dimension into policy development, as this essential level of knowledge is unfortunately often forgotten in higher political analysis (Neveu 2010). We also have a lot to learn from indigenous communities and how they come together and act on their collective responsibility and promote community development. I have learned significantly from many communities, but here I would like to highlight one, and that is Kitigan Zibi Anishinabeg, an Algonquin First Nation community in Quebec, Canada. This community developed a plan with a vision statement that is written in a way that affirms Anishinabeg power to create change. The plan also focuses on its internal moral authority, essentially meaning promoting accountability from within by creating and implementing an internal agenda that motivates and enables all community members to contribute to sustainable success (Kitigan Zibi 2012). The community's leadership is committed to being internally accountable to community members, and the themes of transparency and accountability are strengthened with a renewed focus on reporting to the community on measures that matter to them as well as measures that matter to their funders. As noted in the plan, "We decide how our resources will be used, what actions will be taken and what goals are worthy of our time and effort and those goals come from *within* the community" (Kitigan Zibi 2012). As a result, Kitigan Zibi has become a Center of Excellence in Aboriginal governance, and they offer training and courses to other communities who have shown an interest in their approach. This particular community plan demonstrates the effectiveness of connecting with the collective responsibility to effect change. Government departments and agencies have much to learn from such collective efforts and how sustainable community development requires leaders, policy makers, and citizens to meaningfully engage and work together. This community plan exemplifies the possible intersection where top-down, federal and grassroots, community processes meet. What inspires me is that despite a long history of colonialism and dependency on government and external accountability alone, the Kitigan Zibi Anishnabeg's internal moral authority is alive and well.

NAKED HUMANITY WITHIN AN ETHICAL SPACE

I have found relevance and resonance in the work of Willie Ermine (2007), an indigenous scholar and artist, and his approach on creating an ethical space. The ethical space that my indigenous partners and I have created promotes a language of possibility and allows for 'naked humanity,' where one can just be. Ermine (2000, 121) defines it as the intersection where two or more worlds meet and overlap and thus promote the transformation of knowledge due to alternate knowledge systems being shared, demonstrated through meaningful dialogue. This space is where two distinct communities meet and learn from their cultural differences, and mutual respect for each other's humanity transcends the differences. For instance, bureaucrats can gain significant insight from communities like Kitigan Zibi, where intersections are made between the government's expectations and requirements and the community's, yet the community plan remains community owned and driven. By learning from communities and validating their approach to community development, the counterproductive power dynamic is undone, and common ground or an ethical space is created. In therapy as in the field, the space we form is one of negotiation and intersections created between different systems of knowledge and different value systems (Kirmayer, Rousseau, et al. 2008). When I facilitated cross-cultural engagement among federal representatives from various departments and representatives from remote First Nation communities, an ethical space naturally formed characterized by cultural bridging, which came with its own challenges but with open and honest dialogue, relationships were built. The federal representatives felt less detached and more connected to their purpose in contributing to these particular communities' needs, and the community representatives felt that they were finally being heard.

As in my therapeutic practice, my current work with indigenous partners, and like the space created in the Kumik, the ethical space is where "the presence of the other is acknowledged, but it is space between people, at the unstated, unseen level of thought and feeling . . ." (Ermine 2007, 195), which I refer to as tacit knowledge. This tacit knowledge takes precedence, and it helps define the authentic human-to-human interaction, authentic to self and other that takes place in this ethical space. When book knowledge and my clinical experience prove insufficient, I seek and thrive on this tacit knowledge, which I gain from the mentoring and guidance obtained from my Elders. Such an approach requires compassion, fervor, and a sense of engagement (Archetti 1997), as well as candor and respect. Creating such a space is a form of moral action that could not be disassociated from one's whole mode of being, a mode of life, and a relationship to one's self (Mattingly 2012). Like Lambek (2010), I too believe that ethics *is* intrinsically ordinary as we engage in ethics in our daily lives. My experience has been that being ethical, transparent, and accountable in my daily affairs and interactions is not as complex as it is made to be by some anthropologists, philosophers, and other theorists and practitioners. Rather than create dichotomous and distinct categories of moral discourse versus critical analysis (Fassin 2008) in the study of ethics, where the former simplifies ethics and the latter renders the complexity of issues and approaches, I think it is more relevant and effective to carefully analyze each individual case or research area and tailor a code of ethics to fit the world that we as practitioners encounter (Wedel 2009, 18). The relationship between ethical values and practice is a dynamic one where "values are continuously changing and adapting through actual choices and practices, while, at the same time, they continue to inform and shape choices and practices" (Howell 1997, 4). To listen, empathize, establish trust, and learn from the exchange of knowledge and experience that emanates from the space created by two human beings is how I practice being ethical.

FROM AN ASYMMETRICAL TO A SYMMETRICAL SPACE

Creating an ethical space can be challenging particularly when one is faced with mistrust and apprehension. The reason that the historical dimension of indigenous-Western relations has been defined by a repetitive pattern of connect and disconnect, engagement and disengagement is because the relationship is not founded on human-to-human connection, an equal-level playing field (Ermine 2007, 196). The undercurrent of dominant-oppressed relations remains active in both the Western and indigenous mind-sets. This legacy of dominance and social inequity is definitely part of the status quo in Canada, which is rooted in policies of forced assimilation, and these policies, as Ermine contends, are human constructions. Thus, if we constructed these policies in the past, we have the power to construct policies that foster a new partnership founded on an ethical space and with a cooperative spirit. As illustrated in chapter 3, I too experienced this challenge in confronting the resistance of patients and informants, but as I exuded my authenticity, transparency, and expressed my willingness to learn from the other, the experience transformed to a respectful, ethical space. As a clinician, this space was conducive to healing. As a bureaucrat, this space is conducive to learning. In both, it is about understanding one's humanity through the humanity of another (Ben-Ari and Strier 2010).

Western dominance has impeded the fullest development of the humanity of *both* indigenous and Western peoples. Indigenous people lost their freedom to be themselves, and Westerners lost the opportunity to interact, learn from, and enrich their humanity through building relationships with our indigenous neighbors. I agree with Ermine (2007, 200) that "the plight of indigenous peoples, should act as a mirror to mainstream Canada. [The mirror] . . . is about the character and honor of a nation to have created such conditions of inequity." The challenge for Westerners is to confront this fundamental truth about its own character and learn from our past mistakes and connect with our collective ethical responsibility. In confronting this truth, Western researchers should appropriate the methodologies that talk about reclaiming, recentering, and renaming indigenous nations (Ermine 2000, 105–106). Ermine (2000) contends that it is also the ethical duty of indigenous peoples to find ways to emancipate Western researchers from the grips of colonialist research frameworks and discourse. Collectively, it is our responsibility to ensure that we do not unintentionally or inadvertently promote intergenerational colonialism. We need to take responsibility as an intergenerational moral community (James 2009). Creating that ethical space, a refuge of possibility, and shifting the status quo of an asymmetrical social order to one of partnership (Ermine 2007) are pivotal elements of the decolonization and rehumanization processes and instrumental for reconciliation to transpire. What worked in the past was a nation-to-nation relationship, a partnership existed and it was founded on mutual respect and sharing. The mainstream society needs to create the legal, policy, and social space recognizing the indigenous inherent right of self-determination (Palmater 2014). Colonialism erased indigenous sense of place (Alfred and Corntassel 2005), thus, in order to decolonize and rehumanize and grant the indigenous people's basic right to experience a sense of place, we as settler-allies need to listen, learn from our shared history and painful legacy (Alfred 2005). I would add that we also need to deconstruct our national metanarrative to show that Canada was not a place of peace but one where injustices did occur, and still do. The challenge is that we need to turn our faces toward the truths of injustice, complicities, and contradictions (Davis 2010, 9). In restorying our history, we will be better able to support indigenous people to reclaim their sense of place through cultural resurgence.

REDISCOVERING THE SOUL OF ANTHROPOLOGY

Anthropology is about creating that ethical space that promotes possibilities through intersections, respectful dialogic exchange, openness, reciprocity, and mutual reflection, and so defining anthropology as a moral science of possibilities (Carrithers 2005) for me captures the soul of anthropology—the contingencies, serendipity, complexity, ambiguity, the human-to-human intersubjectivity framed by ethical responsibility. The moral obligations inherent in anthropology make it the most humanistic science. A more human-oriented study conducted in cooperation with the humans under study will go "a long way to help solve not only some of our methodological dilemmas but also our ethical ones" (A. Geertz 1994, 21). As I have shown, anthropology allows for interdisciplinary engagements, which prove to be fruitful for the anthropologist and the informants. My patients, colleagues, and I experience the interdisciplinary engagement between art therapy and anthropology, transcultural psychiatry and anthropology, and such engagements allow for a space where each discipline learns from the other. Such interdisciplinary engagement also allows for the translation of work within one discipline to enrich another discipline. My patient-centered, narrative-based therapy was translated into my work as a government policy advisor to find ways to better and more effectively support community-based initiatives. Similarly, anthropological analysis and ethnographies can enrich a philosophical understanding of ethics (Lambek 2010). Anthropology of public policy should focus on how applied anthropology can enable cross-cultural connections between government and communities because at end of the day both want better outcomes with respect to health and socioeconomic conditions.

I recall a presentation I gave at the University of Genoa in Italy in 2003 on my work with the Quebec Cree as an art therapist/anthropologist. I had a very large audience, and they were motivated to hear more about the history of colonialism in Canada. Many voiced their shock that such cultural oppression happened in a country like Canada. The most common question was why such injustices had occurred in a First World country and why such Third World conditions were still prevalent in many indigenous communities. Another concern was why anthropologists like me were not more actively engaged in the sociopolitical terrain bringing the injustices to the forefront in hopes to effect change. In Europe, there is a strong tradition of anthropological public intellectuals engaged in the sociopolitical arena and bringing anthropology to the public. Scheper-Hughes (2009) claims that anthropologists should also use public issues to influence anthropological thinking and practice; and like she has, anthropologists should create public issues and not simply respond to them. "If anthropology cannot be put to service as a tool for human liberation why are we bothering with it at all? A public anthropology can play its part in all these developments: it has an opportunity to become an arbiter of emancipatory change not just within the discipline, but for humanity itself" (Scheper-Hughes 2009, 3).

MY ETHICAL STANCE

As a clinician, I deconstructed the doctor-patient power dynamic, erased the pretentiousness and the hermeneutics of suspicion, and replaced it with a hermeneutics of trust (Kirmayer 2013) and created common ground. I challenged the "expert position/dynamic" by validating the voices of my patients and actively embracing uncertainty. My ethical stance was to not trump the patient's own self-understanding or silence my patient. I too argue for a broader role for clinicians, not simply as medical expert but as an advocate and partner with patients (Kirmayer 2013, 370). In the early years of my career as an art therapist, I worked in a First Nation community that was then in an extreme state of crisis. I started an art therapy program in the elementary schools, as part of an outreach program in the community center, as well as art therapy clinic for seniors in the community hospital. The leaders in the community asked me to not publish any of the case material or any part of my clinical experience from this community. I kept my word and withheld publishing the rich case material that would have undoubtedly contributed to my career as an art therapist and anthropologist. However, what was of utmost importance to me was to respect the promise made as this nurtured my ethical obligations to this particular community. I recall several colleagues confronting me and questioning me for keeping my word, and I was so disturbed by their lack of integrity. Interestingly, as mentioned in chapter 1, while engaged in my research in transcultural psychiatry where I examined the cultural relevance of a psychiatric construct (Ferrara 1999), I was reprimanded by a psychiatrist who felt I was not respecting the code of conduct of psychiatry. From his perspective, psychiatric constructs have been developed to assess and treat conditions of the psyche that affect an individual's mental health, and they can be applied cross-culturally. Essentially, he did not see the value in my questioning the application of a Western-based construct onto Cree patients. I am truly hoping that this particular psychiatrist has since rethought his approach and reconsidered the importance of cultural qualifications. My definition of an ethical code of conduct is the capacity to know what harms or enhances the well-being of others, and so, in my view, applying a construct or diagnosis without any consideration of the patient's cultural identity is an unethical practice that can be harmful and promote negative implications. Like Levinas (1998), I believe an ethical standard should be compassionately informed as ethics is a practice where one is socially responsible for the other as well as responsible for one's own self-awareness. Throughout my career, I have always placed emphasis on culture as a critical social determinant of health, as recognition and respect for culture are essential to human identity and well-being and so should be considered as fundamental human rights (Kirmayer et al. 2011).

Jorgensen (1971, 322) reminds us that ethical activity involves making choices and adopting a criterion of judgment, and I do not regret sustaining my commitment, my choice to not publish ethnographic case material from this community. We also need to connect with the impact we have on communities and how we affect people in the communities we work in (Jorgensen 1971). When I would travel to communities to hold my art therapy clinics, I would ensure that supports were in place before I left the community. I would work closely with the case workers, and we would assess the existing community resources that they would be able to access when necessary. Oftentimes, in communities that were in crisis, the resources were either limited or unknown as the community was not ready yet to engage in the healing process. In those cases, I worked closely with community case workers, Elders, teachers, and band councillors and brought them together, encouraged dialogue so that when I left, they were drawn to working together. I never went into a community, held my clinic, and left without recognizing the repercussions of my presence and my efforts to facilitate the healing process. My message to each community in crisis was always that the healing had to come from within the community, not from me or another clinician, or from a government program. Another effective support for many communities was facilitating a First Nation–to–First Nation mentoring,[5] where communities would learn from other communities and be often inspired communities to assess and map their own skills and strengths leading to developing their community plan or response. This experience would also help reduce their feelings of isolation and increase their sense of ownership. Like any community development initiative, the healing process has to be community led and community driven. I left each community with the hope that my message would one day resonate. Moreover, my ethical commitment did not halt when I left each community. For me, it only intensified.

An Innu Elder, Sue, recently shared this insight with me: "Recognize, reflect on and appreciate the effects you have on communities. Don't forget the past and what we went through in residential schools." I believe this is a crucial reminder for bureaucrats as many think we are so far from communities; however, the policies we develop clearly affect people in communities, so we are not as far as we may think, as the legacy of the residential school policy has shown us. As Menzies (2010, 64), an indigenous scholar and member of the Sagamok First Nation community claims, "the impact of public policy has left a legacy of trauma within individuals, their families, communities and across nations." We need to stay connected with the past so we do not repeat the same mistakes. In the Indigenous Community Development training, we also place emphasis on learning about trauma and what it is and how intergenerational trauma is a reasonable response and it requires a community response (First Nations and Inuit Health Branch 2013). There is definitely a direct causal relationship between government policy of colonialism and social suffering in indigenous communities. The social and health problems are a logical result of a situation wherein people respond or adapt to unresolved colonial injustices (Alfred 2009; Menzies 2010). In some indigenous communities, it has become a multigenerational way of being, and the effects of a colonially generated cultural disruption become normalized. Thus, it is important that bureaucrats become trauma-informed, just as it is important for health care providers, helping professionals, and anthropologists working in indigenous communities. The better we are informed of trauma, what it looks like, how individuals interpret and experience trauma, the better we are equipped to support their healing process. In relation to indigenous communities, the trauma targeted them because of their indigenous cultural identity and the 'cultural wounding' they experienced, and therefore, we need to recognize that communities need to heal from this targeted trauma (First Nations and Inuit Health Branch 2013). Along with this knowledge and awareness, self-examination, self-reflection is as fundamental to our work as bureaucrats if we are to engage in moral practice with ethical substance.

I went into the field with a work ethic, compassion, and empathy, which are elements of my personal integrity and my internal code of simply being. I was taught the specific professional code of ethics, particular to each profession I engaged in, but in the end, what is most instrumental and fundamental is how I articulate my moral sensibility and my integrity. What helps transform, influence the evolution of my personal work ethic is my daily interactions with others, indigenous and nonindigenous, through our dynamic relationships. By engaging in dialogue and creating that ethical space with my indigenous partners, I am expanding my imagination of what it is to be human rather than viewing others from a distant, disengaged, and uninformed view of their life experiences (Kirmayer, Guzder, and Rousseau 2014). By keeping my word, connecting with my personal mission to effect change, learning and gaining insight from my mistakes, I am being ethically responsible. Educating others about the history of indigenous-Western relations, sharing the truth of residential school survivors, and raising the profile of their resilience and efforts of cultural revitalization define my ethical obligations. As a bureaucrat, I believe in engaging with and continuously forming my ethical subjectivity through my relationship with others.

NOTES

1. Heinz Kohut (1978) believed that conventional scientific methodology was "experience-distant," isolated from human life and experience. Thus, he proposed an "experience-near" approach as an alternative, in which data is acquired directly from empathy and introspection. Kohut maintained that we should strive for an empathic science. Similarly, Abraham Maslow believed an empathic approach should contribute to and enhance conventional science not reduce it (Maslow 1966). Several anthropologists like Wikan (2012) apply the experience-near approach in their work producing rich ethnographies.

2. I agree with Lambek (2010) in that Levinas deserves greater attention in the anthropological analysis of ethics.

3. The South African saying, *umuntu ngumuntu ngabuntu* refers to people are people only through other people (Govier 2003). The South African Truth and Reconciliation Commission was founded on the ubuntu philosophy, and it applied the restorative justice principles, focusing on understanding, reparation, and reconciliation (Forget 2003). Restorative justice looks at crime as representing an interpersonal conflict, thus recognizing, acknowledging, and understanding the victims' life experiences of oppression affect the well-being of the community as a whole.

4. The definition of Elder varies from nation to nation. Elders are chosen based on "their experience as mediators, their spiritual and traditional knowledge, and their capacity to pass on these experiences to others" (A. A. Canada 2010).

5. In the Aboriginal Affairs and Northern Development of Canada regional office in British Columbia, a First Nation–to–First Nation mentorship initiative was recently designed, and it pairs experienced community planners with those just starting out. Annual Comprehensive Community Planning workshops are organized for First Nations to support the development of tools and resources and provide hands-on facilitation and governance support to communities.

Chapter Eight

Conclusion

Towards Intergenerational Reconciliation

My passion to seek meaningful intersections continues to drive my daily efforts, my work as an applied anthropologist and advocate. I channel this passion by organizing and engaging in cross-cultural exchanges and think-tank symposia with federal, provincial, and territorial representatives as well as indigenous community members. As mentioned earlier, when I had organized a meeting of this kind in order to explore how best we can support the quality of life in remote, First Nation and Métis communities, the exchange, the discussion, and the relationships built as a result of this meeting were beyond fruitful. The isolation factor for these remote communities in particular has decreased, and all are aware that sustaining the working relationships requires intent and dedicated time, but when the interchange occurred, all felt like they were being heard. For the government representatives, listening to the indigenous community members allowed them to connect with the reality that the policies they develop have a direct effect on individuals in communities. Even during the Indigenous Community Development training, I find it quite powerful when bureaucrats connect with their purpose and the fact that their efforts can truly make a difference in people's lives, including their own. Such efforts in relationship building and self-reflection translate into the meaning of reconciliation. We need to go beyond hollow, symbolic gestures, which are referred to as cheap reconciliation (Corntassel and Holder 2008). Cheap and meaningless reconciliation promotes the cycle of colonial violence and the culture of denial. Words without action are empty gestures that dismiss and further marginalize indigenous people and promote exclusion.

THE DECLARATION

The United Nations Declaration on the Rights of Indigenous Peoples (UN-DRIP) is viewed by many indigenous and nonindigenous people as a blue-print for justice and reconciliation (General Assembly of the United Nations 2008). As a non-legally binding document, it includes forty-six articles reflecting individual and collective rights of indigenous peoples with respect to culture, identity, language, employment, health, and education. The objective of the UNDRIP is to support the partnership and collaboration with indigenous peoples to eliminate human rights violations against the 370 million indigenous peoples in the world. Canada initially voted against the United Nations' adoption of the UNDRIP in 2007, as did New Zealand, Australia, and the United States, over legal concerns. Canada's greatest concern was the provisions with respect to lands, territories, and resources, and how Canada's constitutional framework protects Aboriginal rights, which include both the Charter of Rights and Freedoms and Section 35 of the Constitution. After careful consideration and discussions with Aboriginal leaders, Canada endorsed the UNDRIP in November 2010. Canada can interpret the articles in the UNDRIP in a manner that is consistent with the nation's constitutional framework. The UNDRIP does not necessarily reflect customary international law or change Canadian laws. However, Canada believes that the UNDRIP has the potential to contribute positively to the promotion and respect of the rights of indigenous peoples around the world (A. A. Canada 2012). What remained the same is Canada's view of the UNDRIP as an aspirational document. As de Costa (2014) notes, the UNDRIP has many ramifications for state policies as it is a human rights instrument that may be used by the Courts to determine outcomes.

Although I view the UNDRIP as a critical instrument in the decolonization process, indigenous scholarship and activism are even more crucial. An indigenous scholar and lawyer, Chelsea Vowel, recently presented on indigenous rights at the International Human Rights Conference at McGill University.[1] Interestingly, she claims that human rights are not an indigenous concept; what is more relevant is the notion of reciprocal obligations—what we owe, and what is owed to us. Czyzewski (2011) also notes how rights have been criticized as an essentially Western concept. Vowel elaborated further by saying, "We are born with an obligation to the land. We cannot give it away, we do not own it. We have a relationship with the land." Similar to Canada's position, Vowel views the UNDRIP as an aspirational document.

Activism such as the Idle No More movement (Idle No More 2013) in Canada is critical in terms of harnessing the power of indigenous voices and educating the Canadian public. Idle No More is a recent protest movement to raise awareness about social and economic conditions experienced by many indigenous people in Canada. This movement contributes to the cultural resurgence as its vision is rooted in indigenous notions of sovereignty and nationhood, social justice, and stewardship and respect for land (Wotherspoon and Hansen 2013). Idle No More is a manifestation of resistance to colonialism, and it accentuates the need to support social inclusion. It is also a reminder for all researchers and policy makers to connect with their ethical responsibility to uphold indigenous views and aspirations, and to develop research and policies in collaboration with indigenous peoples.

At a recent symposium on reconciliation held in Ottawa, Canada, a panel of Chief Commissioners from various provincial and territorial human rights commissions described a framework of reconciliation. This framework defines various elements of reconciliation as follows: 1) political reconciliation (the recognition of two sovereignties); 2) legal reconciliation (recognition of indigenous rights); 3) socioeconomic reconciliation (ensure that all indigenous people experience the same opportunities and living conditions as others); 4) spiritual reconciliation (recognition of cultural diversity among indigenous peoples). I appreciate how reconciliation is deconstructed in this framework, and this multifaceted description can definitely be presented in our educational efforts to support the momentum toward intergenerational reconciliation. At this same symposium, International Chief Wilton Littlechild noted in his keynote address that the UNDRIP, which he prefers to call 'the Declaration,' is an instrument of reconciliation. In his words, "Reconciliation is about having good relations, *wetaskiwin*, in Cree. It is about building individual-to-individual relations as well as organization-to-organization relations. Reconciliation entails a systemic change, which takes time." And so, in his view, the Declaration provides the foundation in the form of principles, to work better together to preserve indigenous cultural heritage and support indigenous visions of sustainable, socioeconomic development. Interestingly on September 20, 2014, the Canadian Museum for Human Rights will opened in Winnipeg, Manitoba on Treaty One land, the historical location of the Métis occupation. Inspiring human rights reflection and dialogue is one of the museum's guiding principles. The museum demonstrates a concrete example of reconciliation and how we can work together and learn from each other. In developing its exhibits, the museum gathered input from Elders and community members, as well as indigenous experts, scholars, artists, curators, and human rights experts. The museum is working with a Standing Indigenous Advisory Council to ensure that a range of indigenous perspectives inform the museum's work. Indigenous content is found in each of the museum's ten core galleries, and it is especially showcased in the Indigenous Perspectives gallery. The stories of indigenous rights involve human rights violations and resistance. The purpose of the indigenous narratives is to share and connect them to Canada and the historic and ongoing human rights issues around the world (Canadian Museum for Human Rights 2014).[2]

A SENSE OF AGENCY AND URGENCY

Each applied anthropologist in the field of indigenous studies has to define their commitment; own their process, knowledge, and self-awareness; and experience a sense of agency. If we are to support community development and we expect communities to gain a sense of agency, then we should mirror this and adopt this expectation for ourselves. I am inspired by communities who have identified with a sense of agency of their own cultural revitalization and healing process, and they inspire me to do the same—to own my role in the reconciliation process. I speak with authority with respect to reconciliation because of the urgency it necessitates. I believe that there is an urgency of the predicament being faced by indigenous people whose cultural identities have been deeply wounded, and I am personally committed to respond compassionately to this urgency. I welcome those who embrace this urgency and those who are ready to walk the path of reconciliation alongside our indigenous neighbors, recognizing our common humanity, learning from our differences, and promoting social inclusion. I too set forth an urgent appeal for us all, indigenous and nonindigenous, to connect with our responsibilities as human beings to learn from the past; understand it at the cognitive, affective, and spiritual levels; and work in solidarity toward a more sustainable future (Davis 2010). Having wounded indigenous cultural identities demands moral reparation, and so I strongly believe that the moral and ethical obligation of each and every nonindigenous Canadian is to own the residential school legacy and history (Crean 2009). The necessary first in moral reform is to acknowledge exploitation and injustice (Prager and Govier 2003), especially by nonindigenous people who have lived in denial for so long. We need to propel an intergenerational moral responsibility to fulfill our collective obligation to indigenous people to support healthy identity formation and a sense of belongingness.

Another injustice that requires an immediate sense of agency and urgency is the missing and murdered indigenous women in Canada. Indigenous women make up 4.3 percent of the Canadian population but account for 16 percent of female homicides and 11.3 percent of missing women—this speaks to the severity and urgency of this issue. Between 1980 and 2012, there were 1,181 cases—164 were missing women and 1,017 homicide victims, all of which are indigenous (RCMP 2014). In March 2014, the report from the Members of Parliament on the Special Committee on Violence against Indigenous Women tabled recommendations after hearing sixty-one witness testimonials (Parliament of Canada 2014). The report entitled, *Invisible Women: A Call to Action*, recommended a public awareness and prevention campaign and the implementation of a national DNA-based missing person's index. A national inquiry was not recommended; however, the report proposed that the federal government implement all the recommendations through a coordinated action plan. In May 2014, the Royal Canadian Mounted Police (RCMP) completed a national operational review or detailed statistical breakdown, and it is considered the most comprehensive data that has ever been collected by the Canadian policing community on missing and murdered Aboriginal women (RCMP 2014). RCMP argues that the vast majority of these cases are addressed through police investigation, and they have been enhancing efforts on unresolved cases, as well as increasing attention on prevention efforts. The Canadian Human Rights Commission, indigenous leaders, activists, and opposition leaders in the federal government have been asking for a national public inquiry to explore the root causes of so many deaths and disappearances; many feel that if these missing and murdered women were of any other ethnic origin in Canada, the federal government approach would be different. The Canadian Human Rights Commission believes that this is one of the most pressing human rights issue facing Canada today (Canadian Human Rights Commission 2014). Oxfam Canada has referred to this injustice as an "epidemic of femicide," noting that Canada as a country has yet to deal with its legacy of colonialism (The Independent, August 24, 2014).

Overall, the federal government believes that this reality should be viewed as a crime rather than a sociological phenomenon. I believe all crime should be considered as sociological phenomena, and these missing and murdered women are a direct result of intergenerational trauma caused by colonialism. The RCMP report also noted that there are challenging socioeconomic circumstances that need to be considered. I argue that we need more culturally based initiatives to support the healing process so that indigenous people have the opportunity to reconnect and restore their cultural identities rather than be further marginalized. We also need to support national organizations like the Native Women's Association of Canada, the Pauktuutit Inuit Women's Association, and research initiatives that are culturally relevant, such as the Sisters in Spirit (Spirit 2009). The report completed by the Sisters in Spirit initiative in 2009 should be considered as a valuable, foundational research study that can help inform policy development. It is a community-based initiative using a life-story methodology through interviews, and it illustrates four key policy areas that require attention:

1. The reduction of violence against Aboriginal women and girls;
2. The reduction of poverty, which will increase the safety and security of Aboriginal women;
3. The reduction of homelessness and increased access to safe, secure and affordable housing; and,
4. Improved access to justice for Aboriginal women and their families.

The report illustrates each of these themes in detail. This report speaks to the need for further collaborative work among all levels of government, police forces, and indigenous women's organizations. This is not a government or indigenous or a policing issue but a Canadian one. This is a stark reality that all Canadians need to better understand and a reminder that we be more inclusive and more respectful of indigenous people. Policy makers need to listen to indigenous women, learn from their life experiences and their proposed approaches.

I believe it is most important to take action at this point, and this action needs to be strength-based, founded on indigenous knowledge and culture, and reflective of holistic well-being. Programs should not be developed with a limited focus on mental health or the prevention of substance abuse, for instance; we should apply the framework of social determinants of health and well-being, including physical, emotional, spiritual, and cultural elements. As outlined in chapter 4, programs that are developed and implemented using these guiding principles and framework are the most effective.

I would also like to call for a bicultural approach like the *Whanau Ora*, whole-of-government approach adopted in New Zealand to help improve the Maori health outcomes, where the indigenous people participate in their own culture as well as in the mainstream culture. I always wondered why immigrants, like my own ancestors, were given the space to maintain their language and distinct cultural ways while also actively engaged in the mainstream culture. Why are First Nations, Inuit, and Métis not granted that same space, that same opportunity—that is, to maintain one's cultural identity and acculturate to selective elements of the mainstream culture? This exists in some pockets across North America—for example, in British Columbia where there is a large number of First Nations. However, this is where government at all levels—federal, provincial, or territorial—can work together, play a significant role, and develop policies and tools to support cultural diversity and social inclusion. We should all experience the values transferred from intergenerational wisdom and resilience. And I know that many First Nations, Inuit, and Métis people have missed out on this great opportunity, but hopefully they can choose to connect with other indigenous Elders who, fortunately for us, are still here, ready to share their resilience and their teachings. Indigenous people have survived every genocidal law, policy, and action thrown at them, and they are still here today (Palmater 2014). Thus, regaining their sociocultural integrity is doable as it has yet to be dissolved due to their survival skills and strength in resilience. We as settler-allies need to learn from indigenous people's resilience as we promote intergenerational reconciliation.

I hope to see more interaction, more intersections created based on respect, leading to enriched learning experiences. Reconciliation is about supporting the healing process within communities, community development, as well as supporting indigenous people to contribute to the mainstream society. Reconciliation in my view is also about dismantling or dissolving the marginalization, reducing that sense of isolation while strengthening a sense of belongingness.

Rehumanization and decolonization have to prevail as they are prerequisites to reconciliation. A crucial part of the rehumanization process is to understand the anger, apprehension, and mistrust indigenous people have toward government and validating it. The history is recent, and therefore decolonization will take time, progress will be incremental. There is hope. I have witnessed change, the evolution of a community in crisis to becoming successful, collaborating, and self-sustaining. I work with many compassionate bureaucrats who believe in the urgency reconciliation necessitates. When I get overwhelmed and the progress seems too slow or at times dismal, I turn to my fellow indigenous and nonindigenous colleagues, and especially my Elders. An Elder, an Ojibwe woman, I met many years ago, "Your spirit will get overwhelmed and frustrated so just know that when you teach one, you teach many and when you heal one, you heal many." In whatever position I am in, I will enable the connection from one community to another so that they learn from each other, and I will continue to share my experiential knowledge in hopes to inspire others to learn from the past and learn from each other, indigenous and nonindigenous alike.

With respect to healing, it is critical that a community is able to develop a sense of urgency, a plan for the future, and capacity to take action. Community needs to decide what direction it will go, and as many communities have experienced, healing is a precursor to community development. We, Westerners in particular, should be inspired by community resilience. I have witnessed individuals exhibiting resilience that sometimes leads to community resilience and vice versa, where a community with resilient characteristics promotes resilience in individuals in communities. Community resilience has important implications for efforts to promote holistic well-being, and it also depends on the relationship the community has with the mainstream society and with government institutions. "Addressing the divisive policies and practices in government at all levels and enhancing public knowledge of and respect for Aboriginal cultures, traditions and aspirations is a necessary part of any comprehensive effort to promote community resilience" (Kirmayer, Sehdev et al. 2009, 6). Indigenous people who have healed from multiple trauma and oppression have many lessons on humanity and resilience for all (Lemay, Hopkins, and Couchie 2014). Many of the participants in the Indigenous Community Development training, as well as students and colleagues, are struck by indigenous cultural resilience. For example, a First Nation community organized a birthday party for all residential school victims who had passed away and their truths buried with them. This event had such impact that it became a transition point for the community's healing process.

I strongly believe that those who are nonindigenous may have something to learn about healing that is based on the strength of culture. A victim-centered approach tends to pathologize indigenous people; a strength-centered approach focuses on the community and indigenous knowledge, and it is culture-based. Community development is not a stand-alone program nor a stand-alone policy (First Nations and Inuit Health Branch 2013). We need to embed community development knowledge, principles, and expertise across the federal departments in every policy and program. We in government should ask ourselves how this policy or program we are drafting or channelling through the bureaucratic system supports a community-centered and culture, strength-based approach. We need to openly and actively engage with communities to ensure that policy is not solely driven by bureaucratic goals of efficiency and expediency but that policy is especially reflective of communal aspirations and allows for flexibility in the translation of policy on the ground. Interestingly, what I have noticed is that government is such an active player in community development but rarely admits it.

THE POTENTIAL OF ADAPTIVE POLICIES

I strongly believe in the potential and possibilities of the development of adaptive policies, as illustrated in chapter 4 in my presentation of place-based approach. Adaptive policies, as defined by Swanson and Bhadwal (2009), enable the self-organization and social networking capacity of communities; promote variation in policy responses as well as formal policy review and continuous learning through engagement between government and community, which is applied to evolving policies. For the "cynical bureaucrat," at first glance this development process may not be considered possible or may be an intangible option. However, as we saw in chapter 4, adaptive policies or a place-based approach is highly probable. The process needs to be founded on integrated and forward-looking analysis, multistakeholder deliberation, as well as monitoring key performance indicators in order to adjust the policy accordingly so it is more responsive to community needs (Swanson and Bhadwal 2009, 15). Like Irlbacher-Fox (2009, 169), I too believe that the recognition of ongoing injustice can lead to viable policy alternatives that are more reflective of lived realities. The Supreme Court of Canada may propel all governments—federal, provincial, and territorial—to rethink their roles and responsibilities and develop more adaptive policies to better support indigenous sustainable community development.

As bureaucrats, the reality we need to embrace is unknown unknowns in the policy-making world especially one that is responsive to community members. Rather than policies being viewed as static objects, they should be seen as organic and evergreen, with the capacity to adapt to both anticipated and unanticipated conditions. Engaging in the development of adaptive policies allows bureaucrats to see their role in investing in responsive, sustainable community development. "Designers and implementers of adaptive policies embrace the uncertainty and complexity of policy context, and consider learning, continuous improvement and adaptation of the policy a natural part of the policy life-cycle" (Swanson and Bhadwal 2009, 15). Learning is ongoing and continuous and does not end when one obtains a doctorate or after twenty or thirty years in the public service.[3] I recall sitting in a boardroom meeting, and I wondered out loud how can we better work together and break down the silos. I suggested that we at Aboriginal Affairs and Northern Development Canada learn from Aboriginal communities that were engaged in community planning and develop an internal community plan ourselves. The immediate response from one of my colleagues was, "But we are not a community, so how would that work?" I totally disagree, as an intra-type community plan[4] would be in my eyes a strategic, evergreen think piece that would allow us to focus on our assets, our weaknesses, and learn to more effectively work together rather than expend so much energy in our silos, which does not benefit us as a federal government department nor does it benefit communities and the people we serve. Such a departmental community plan would be inspired by community resilience. If we are developing policies to support reconciliation, we need to integrate indigenous knowledge to exemplify our renewed commitment to building relationships, to collaborate, and to ensure that policies reflect the collaborative efforts, that they are not just one-sided or created from top-down. And for those communities who are doing extremely well, engaged in sustaining their progress, government should not get out of their way but should learn from them in order to more effectively support other communities.

THE POWER OF INDIGENOUS KNOWLEDGE

My personal bias is I view indigenous knowledge and their ways of seeing the world as having such potential to rescue our basic humanity. Indigenous leaders and scholars and community knowledge have become "the space of hope and possibility for Indigenous Peoples" (Ermine 2000, 89). Indigenous knowledge, values, and perspectives have a crucial role in the development of community resilience (Kirmayer, Sehdev et al. 2009, 75). I was in Labrador several years ago working with the Mushua Innu, and we had organized an extracurricular program where we had combined cultural activities and group art therapy sessions with Elders and youth as participants. During our walk in the woods looking for tea leaves, I was so focused on looking around, scared that a bear would surprise us, and then the Elder looked at me and said, "You need to look down and appreciate what is at your feet. You

would be amazed at what the Creator has left for us so close to the ground."
Once again, the rich simplicity that this message conveyed, stemming from
this Elder's common sense both stunned and inspired me for many reasons.
Firstly, I was thankful and will be forever grateful that the indigenous cosmologies and ways of being have survived colonialism. Secondly, I feel
fortunate that I continue to witness cultural revitalization. Thirdly, I strongly
believe indigenous knowledges have the power to enable emancipatory
change with Western academia and sciences and facilitate the path toward a
more empathic approach to scientific investigation. This emancipatory
change may foster more open-mindedness and readiness to embrace such an
empathic approach and appreciate its value, its impact, and its benefit. Interestingly, and I see value in Ermine's (2000) argument, that indigenous peoples should find ways to emancipate Western researchers from the grips of
Western research frameworks and discourse. He claims this as the moral and
ethical duty of indigenous peoples. "Indigenous scholars are perhaps in the
best position to chart the appropriate pathways to emancipating and transforming knowledge. The critical indigenous scholar can readily occupy the
ethical space that is characterized as the confluence of two worldviews"
(Ermine 2000, 120). Similarly, White, Maxim, and Beavon (2003) argue that
indigenous scholars can use their greater cultural understanding and personal
histories to address many of the research gaps that plague the Aboriginal
policy domain. What the domain of science needs is more indigenous scientists and more strategic partnerships between indigenous and nonindigenous
scientists to find real solutions to real problems (White, Maxim, and Beavon
2003).

Indigenous scientists, in my eyes, are practicing the values of empathic
scientific research. Although considered a new movement among Western
scientists (cf. Rifkin 2009), many indigenous scholars and scientists have
bridged human compassion and technical, research expertise. Like Alfred
(2005) and Ermine (2000, 2007), both indigenous scholars, I agree that what
is blatantly missing in Western approaches is the reluctance and ambivalence
toward integrating the cognitive and affective domains of research. What we
as Western social scientists have much to learn is that empathic research is
where the researcher's reflexive experience informs the process, enriches
science in general, and does not reduce it. Cultural competence requires one
to be self-aware of one's own cultural identity, values, and beliefs, to have
intent to develop one's knowledge base of how history has impacted our
current realities in this country, and requires relational skills to provide cultural safety to a client of a different culture.

Cultural competence goes both ways—to better understand the settler
culture as well as indigenous cultures. I often think of the relevance of an
Iroquois legend I would hear often while working in Iroquois communities,
and interestingly I heard it again recently while working in government. The

legend is of the first settlers and how the First Peoples and Europeans would each paddle in their respective canoes and they would respect each other and their way forward. Clearly that did not continue for long as Europeans oppressed the native people of this land and colonialism prevailed leading to intergenerational trauma. In moving forward and engaging in social change while preserving historical memory, reconciliation is about rebuilding relationships between indigenous and nonindigenous framed by the essence of this legend, that is, to seek and nurture peaceful and respectful coexistence— at least, I know that it defines the ultimate goal of my personal mission. This legend reminds us that the history is *our* history, settlers and indigenous people. It also symbolizes the meaning behind the treaties made between Europeans and the indigenous peoples. Perhaps we need to review and reconsider the original intent of the treaties. As Boldt (1993, 116) clearly sets forth, the paradigm shift that has to occur is that policies must be developed with equitable reference to indigenous rights, interests, needs, and aspirations and must speak to the spirit of coexistence, mutual obligation, sharing, and benefit that defined the treaties. We in government can learn from other initiatives that have been built within a balanced, respectful framework, such as the International Initiative for Mental Health Leadership, which is a strong example of an organization that protects indigenous perspectives and builds understanding between indigenous and nonindigenous peoples (Lemay et al. 2014, 7). It is also critical to give more attention to young indigenous leaders, who are more in favor of enduring relationships rather than quick solutions. In the winter of 2013, a group of six Cree youth walked 1600 kilometres (or 994 miles) from their northern Quebec Cree community of Whapmagoostui to Parliament Hill in Ottawa with the objective to reconnect with their land and cultural heritage and to raise awareness. When they arrived in Ottawa nine weeks later, the group had increased to four hundred. This movement empowered many of the youth participants, who prior to the walk were feeling depressed and were experiencing suicidal thoughts (Aboriginal 2014), and they felt that the walk helped raise awareness of their Cree community. Youth leaders like these recognize that for reconciliation to take place, the mainstream society has to make room for the assertion of indigenous cultural resurgence (Montour and Huddart 2013).

WHAT'S NEXT FOR ME?

I have a sustained commitment to undo colonial legacies; contribute as an empathic researcher to humanistic anthropology; and support place-based, community-driven policy development where top-down process meets, intersects, and learns from the grassroots perspective. I remain actively engaged in my role as cross-cultural ambassador, liaison, and consciousness raiser. I want to continue to immerse in transformative learning, especially from the spiritual impulse or radical spiritual component of fieldwork (Mahmood 2002). I appreciate and yearn for more experiences in the field that challenge my spirit, trigger my emotions and my intellectual curiosity, compelling me to self-reflect. Nurturing my cultural competence remains in the forefront as it is my lifelong, developmental journey, as well as my ethical responsibility. My daily challenge is to remain aware of my cultural identity and learn from and be open to other cultures, and gain knowledge on the current realities in First Nation, Inuit, and Métis communities. I am committed to applying these principles of cultural competence to my working relationships as the more I network, the better I support community development, and the more I connect with my purpose. Effective education of mainstream policy makers on cultural competence is key to effective outcomes. The Indigenous Community Development team is currently working toward maintaining a community of practice, protecting the integrity of the training, and the quality of the curriculum to ensure a standard of professional commitment and credibility. My work with the training entails creating that ethical space as well as channelling my compassionate informed ethical action into a mindful practice. What I have experienced and continue to is that a collaborative working relationship as well as a clinical encounter is shaped by the moment-to-moment cognizance of values or ethical self-awareness (Epstein 1999, 836).

From a distant view or perspective, my career path may seem bizarre, blurred, and undefined, but interestingly, to many of my indigenous partners it has always made sense. I am fully aware that my work does not fit "easily" within the traditional disciplinary boundaries of a "real anthropology" defined by real fieldwork (Gupta and Ferguson 1997). My location of the field may be considered as an innovative reconceptualization of anthropological fieldwork with a heightened sense of the interrelationships among the social, cultural, and political dynamics of the field. As Gupta and Ferguson (1997, 38) claim, rethinking the field in this sense is part of practicing decolonized anthropology, and ethnographic intervention should be conceived and practiced as a search for truth in the service of universal humanistic knowledge. Nonetheless, those who are not comfortable with such an innovative approach or eclectic background have critiqued me, wondering why I was not practicing 'real anthropology' or contributing to the mainstream domain of science. My approach may be considered similar to Niezen's (2009) in terms on the interdisciplinarity and an articulated sense of the interrelatedness of subject matters of various disciplines. My experience as a psychotherapist has definitely enriched my work as an anthropologist with its focus on listening, empathy, dialogic exchange, and relationship building. My ethnographic skills and cultural competence definitely enriched the treatment plans I developed for my patients. Throughout my career, I have applied my cross-disciplinary lessons learned. I believe there are more advantages than disadvantages to my eclectic background. At one point in my career path, I admit, I had absorbed some of the judgments I had heard by questioning what I was doing, and wondering how perhaps it would have been a less challenging path if I would have chosen to not pursue with my attempts at rethinking, reconstructing, and decolonizing. Those moments thankfully did not last long enough to alter my approach. Now, I see how my life chances and my choices make sense, and how everything has fallen into place. Serendipity, embracing it, being open to it has allowed me to explore elements of my core, my own humanity and learn from others' and their humanity. I continue on my journey to *just be*—with its challenges, the judgments, bumps and bruises, joys, elation and fulfillment, always in hope to inspire others to do the same. I don't place emphasis on how I have been marginalized but more on my purpose, how it has defined my reason for being. Interestingly, what I experienced in First Nation, Inuit, and Métis communities was a sense of belongingness. Never once did I feel marginalized or unwanted. I did experience mistrust in some communities, but my validation of their feelings was key in forming a relationship. This experience of inclusiveness has always inspirited me, and it sustains my passion to give back to indigenous peoples with the hope that they too can experience that fundamental sense of belongingness.

I continue to channel my limitless store of altruism. I honestly do not know how else to describe what I have, whether it is a gift or just a unique idiosyncratic trait of mine—whatever it is, it is there, and I would like to tap into it more so to benefit others as well as myself. Recently, someone told me that it seems like I have lived four lives with everything that I have experienced. This really struck me because of the power attached to the statement and the sense of accomplishment that I have exuded. Personally, I feel like I need to do so much more, and that's what drives me. Daily, I ensure to invigorate and sustain my passion, my advocacy, and remain committed to investing in the well-being of indigenous peoples and connected with the impact I as a compassionate bureaucrat have on communities and their lived realities. The fact that I feel I am making a difference, no matter how measurable, is the most gratifying feeling of all. I feel like I have and continue to contribute to the significant and timely movements of patient-centered and narrative-based treatment approaches, and now actively promote community-centered policy development and a trauma-informed approach all in the spirit of reconciliation.

My clinical experience at an Italian-community hospital allowed me to connect with my own cultural being, and I now believe that when the Elders asked me to bring my healing to my own people, their intention was for me to do just that. "Clinicians who understand something of their own cultural background and how it contributes to their values, perceptions, and personal style are in a better position to learn from the clinical encounter with others"

(Kirmayer, Rousseau et al. 2008, 315). The Elders wanted me to understand the impact of my own cultural identity on my work. While working in an Iroquois First Nation community that was in the healing process and strengthening their connection to their language, a young girl decided to give me a "First Nation name." She named me *Katsitsio*, translated as "beautiful flower." I was so honored and elated I shared this heartfelt gesture with my colleague, who was also my Elder while working there, and in a very calm and serious tone she said, "That is good she said that. It shows she trusts you. But, do not forget who you are. You are not First Nation, you identify with being Italian not First Nation and that's so important. The more you identify with who you are, the better you allow others to identify with who they are." To be honest, her words did not disappoint me nor deflate my elated mood, but what her words did was ground me in who I am, allowing me to reconnect with my humility. My personal attributes of humility, empathy, maturity, energy, determination, and creativity are used to build relationships, listen to the voices and narratives, and raise the profile of these lived narratives whether through an ethnography, in therapy, or in policy development. My humility plays a fundamental role in encouraging the patient then, and the community now to the expert and I the student of the patient or the community with the conviction that we both carry the potential to be a capable and full partner in the reconciliation process (cf. Tervalon and Murray-Garcia 1998). My cultural competence becomes best illustrated by humility as I am willing to build on the individual patient or community's assets and adaptive strengths. And now with the Indigenous Community Development training, with its focus on developing one's cultural competence, emphasis is placed on building one's self-awareness and knowledge and applying both to building effective relationships. This undercurrent was ignited at the beginning of my career and remains active now.

How do I show my gratitude for everything they have given to me and how my life has been so enriched? My answer is this: I continue to nurture my ethical stance, to be an advocate, educate others, and support policy development that is reflective and inclusive of indigenous voices and lived realities. I feel indebted to Luke for igniting my curiosity that evolved into my passion, for inspiring my self-discovery, encouraging me to engage in reflexivity while working rather than making my self-reflection an isolated experience. The serendipity I experienced then perhaps can be best described as two 'accidental wisdoms' connecting, with both chance and sagacity playing a key role (cf. Rivoal and Salazar 2013). For these past twenty-five years, *meegwetch* to Luke and all the indigenous individuals I have met and learned from, and to the nonindigenous partners who are engaged in decolonization and reconciliation, and who see this as a dynamic process that has socioeconomic and cultural implications and benefit for all. I recently received an email from my colleague who is from Kitigan Zibi, a First Nation community in Quebec. For me, it sums up how reconciliation has been made real for me and for those I work closely with. A fundamental prerequisite to getting to this point was building a respectful working relationship and sustaining it. She signed off the email with, "Looking forward to participating in a conversation that amplifies morally independent, self-directing freedom for First Nations." My hope is that our collective efforts create a ripple effect with healing as the contagion in communities and reconciliation as an ongoing process where the "us versus them" dichotomy is a distant memory.

NOTES

1. This conference was held on July 23, 2014, and she followed my presentation on Global Indigenous Rights.

2. The Indigenous Perspectives gallery in the museum demonstrates indigenous-centered perspectives of rights, and their presence and importance in contemporary Canada. It also reflects the vitality and diversity of indigenous peoples across Turtle Island, or what is now called North America. This gallery functions as both an educational space and a space of honor for the indigenous peoples of these vast lands (Canadian Museum for Human Rights 2014).

3. On my first day on the job in government my then-supervisor shook my hand as he introduced himself and told me "Your PhD means nothing here, and it does not come close to my twenty-six years in the public service."

4. This plan is similar to a Strength, Weaknesses, Threats, and Opportunities (SWOT) analysis that is often used in government, but the difference with this plan is that it remains evergreen and an ongoing reference point, and not just a one-time analysis.

.

Epilogue

Coming Home — Bi-Giiwe

My story will never be complete, and what I have presented here is just a snapshot of my journey. My story continues to evolve, reflecting my own personal growth. As a humble individual, this experience of writing an auto-ethnography was quite the challenge, yet it has been cathartic, enriching, and transformative. And now that my story is "out there," I welcome the obstacles and the uncertainty with fear and vulnerability. I fear failure and disappointing others, and I fear the critique that naturally comes with writing and publishing such personal narratives, but I am ready to face these fears in hopes that I inspire at least one individual to connect with their own story. I challenge my fellow anthropologists to consider the value of engaging in an auto-ethnography. I remain grateful for this opportunity to share my story as many did not have such a chance, which propels me to raise the voice of those unheard or those unable to share their narratives. I am also grateful for (and quite comfortable with) not knowing everything, as I yearn to learn and broaden my scope. It is especially difficult at times when others expect me to have the answers given my education and my experience; however, as I want to be authentic in my teachings, I want to be authentic in my quest to learn. My reflexivity, my learning process, my engagement and collaboration remain ongoing. Learning is lifelong, and transformative learning has an impact on me directly and implicitly on others I meet, interact with, while transferring my knowledge.

Learning also entails facing the good, the bad, and the ugly. In order to promote equality, we need to acknowledge the existence of racism, admit this ugly truth, and try to understand what racism looks like from an indigenous point of view. "As far as Aboriginal people are concerned, racism in

Canadian society continues to invade our lives institutionally, systematically, and individually. . . . The heinous violations of human rights which have been perpetuated upon our people for generations merely because of our race, cannot go unmarked" (Fontaine 1998). Historical memory is still being felt. The politically tense postcolonial context remains prevalent, and too often settlers adopt a position of superiority, communicated in an unknowing way. These power imbalances that are inherent in this postcolonial context need to be acknowledged. To create respectful ground and promote inclusiveness, we can apply the principles of the relational theory of restorative justice, which recognizes the fundamental interconnectedness of people (Llewellyn 2008). "Restorative justice resonates with and owes much to the insights of Aboriginal conceptions of justice" (Llewellyn 2008, 188). Restorative processes need to be inclusive, dialogical, and participatory. The most important requirement is the *willingness* of the individuals involved.

We cannot support self-determination and colonial reparations without recognizing that racist beliefs and practices continue in Canada. Thus, our role is to acknowledge, demystify, deconstruct, and re-story our history in collaboration with our indigenous partners. We cannot afford to *not* do this. We all have too much to lose. If we choose to not do this, then such a choice essentially reflects imperial, Western arrogance. "Colonial culture for both the victims and the perpetrators is fundamentally a denial of the past and of its moral implications. It is an aversion to the truth about who we really are and where it is that we came from" (Alfred 2011, 5). Restitution may be the precondition to any form of reconciliation (Alfred 2011); however, before we give back to indigenous peoples in terms of land and rights, we need to establish relationships and claim an authentic, supportive acknowledgment of our shared colonial past. Re-storying entails for us all to take ownership of our colonial history, listen with an empathetic spirit, establish respectful relationships, and engage in critical self-reflection. It is not just about returning to a peaceful coexistence but to move toward a future founded on relationships of equal concern, respect, and dignity. We also need to recognize that the concept of indigeneity and belongingness are intimately entwined. Niezen (2009) argues for a need to better understand the local complexities of indigenous expressions of culture, identity, and belonging. Indigenous peoples are rediscovering themselves and are achieving significant political success through their creative use of contemporary discourses, technologies, and institutions. The resilience of indigenous peoples has remained a constant since the first contact with European settlers. Indigenous people have been successful in surviving, and this reality has to be highlighted in this re-storying as they regain their sense of belongingness, their sense of *place*. Given that colonization and dehumanization impacted seven generations, reconcilation and rehumanization will take time for it to become mainstream, and for all indigenous people to feel like they belong. My wish is that all indigenous people have the chance to showcase their resilience, restore their dignity and their cultural pride.

"The sacrifices of our ancestors require that we, as indigenous peoples, take positive steps to heal our communities and Nations and bring our lost people home" (Palmater 2014, 48).

As an ally, I need and want to support the coming-home process, to ensure that indigenous people experience that sense of belongingess once again. What I offer is my honesty, my respect, my passion to stake claim to restorative justice and enable cultural restoration. I practice my grandparents' teachings by offering my genuine spirit of inquiry that is respectful of the dignity and humanity of others in creating spaces of connection, where committed relationships are developed and sustained (Lederach 2001; Regan 2010). I am proud to be a catalyst for social change especially with respect to non-indigenous people moving from complacency to empathy and beyond detached concern to active engagement. I stand in solidarity with indigenous peoples and fellow North Americans who are committed to discovering ways to belong to this land together, and to bring *our* lost people home.

NOTE

Bi-Giiwe refers to "coming home" in Ojibwe.

.

Bibliography

AAA, American Anthropological Association. *Committee on Public Policy.* May 8, 2009. http://www.aaanet.org/cmtes/ppc/ (accessed November 16, 2013).

Aboriginal, CBC News. *Quebec Cree Walkers Find Lasting Impact in Trek to Ottawa.* April 17, 2014. http://www.cbc.ca/news/aboriginal/quebec-cree-walkers-find-lasting-impact-in-trek-to-ottawa-1.2612958 (accessed August 25, 2014).

Aboriginal Affairs and Northern Development of Canada. *Backgrounder—Income Assistance Reform: Enhanced Service Delivery.* June 12, 2013. http://www.aadnc-aandc.gc.ca/eng/1371048267592/1371048310299 (accessed December 31, 2013).

———. *Fact Sheet: Aboriginal Self-Government.* June 11, 2014. http://www.aadnc-aandc.gc.ca/eng/1100100016293/1100100016294 (accessed October 27, 2014).

———. *Frequently Asked Questions: Canada's Endorsement of the United Nations Declaration on the Rights of Indigenous Peoples.* May 2, 2012. http://www.aadnc-aandc.gc.ca/eng/1309374807748/1309374897928 (accessed July 28, 2014).

———. *Kumik–Council of Elders.* September 15, 2010. http:www.aadnc-aandc.gc.ca/eng/1100100013748/1100100013749 (accessed December 4, 2013).

———. *Remembering the Past: A Window to the Future.* June 11, 2013. https://www.aadnc-aandc.gc.ca/eng/1332859355145/1332859433503 (accessed July 15, 2014).

Aboriginal Healing Foundation. *Aboriginal Healing Foundation.* October 30, 2013. http://www.ahf.ca (accessed November 24, 2013).

Abu-Lughod, Lila. "Writing against Culture." In *Recapturing Anthropology: Working in the Present*, by Richard Fox, 137–162. Santa Fe, NM: School of American Research Press, 1991.

Alfred, Gerald Taiaiake. "Colonialism and State Dependency." *Journal de la Santé Autochtone*, 2009: 42–60.

———. "Colonial Stains on Our Existence." In *Racism, Colonialism, and Indigeneity in Canada*, by Martin J. Cannon and Lina Sunseri, 3–11. Don Mills: Oxford University Press, 2011.

———. *Wasáse: Indigenous Pathways of Action and Freedom.* Toronto: University of Toronto Press, 2005.

Alfred, Taiaiake, and Jeff Corntassel. "Being Indigenous: Resurgences against Contemporary Colonialism." *Government and Opposition*, 2005: 597–614.

Allen-Meares, Paula. "Cultural Competence: An Ethical Requirement." *Journal of Ethnic and Cultural Diversity in Social Work*, 2007: 83–92.

American Anthropological Association. *Professional Ethics.* 2013. http://www.aaanet.org/profdev/ethics/ (accessed December 13, 2013).

Antze, Paul. "On the Pragmatics of Empathy in the Neurodiversity Movement." In *Ordinary Ethics*, by Michael Lambek, 310–327. New York: Fordham University Press, 2010.

Appell, George N. "Scholars, True Believers, and the Identity Crisis in American Anthropology." *Reviews in Anthropology*, 1992: 193–202.

Archetti, Eduardo P. "The Moralities of Argentinian Football." In *The Ethnography of Moralities*, by Signe Howell, 98–123. New York: Routledge, 1997.

Archibald, Linda. *Decolonization and Healing: Indigenous Experiences in the United States, New Zealand, Australia and Greenland.* Report, Ottawa: The Aboriginal Healing Foundation, 2006.

Arnold, Carrie. *New Science Shows How Maggots Heal Wounds.* April 7, 2013. http://www.scientificamerican.com/article.cfm?id=news-science-shows-how-maggots-heal-wounds (accessed November 11, 2013).

Asch, Michael. *Home and Native Land: Aboriginal Rights and the Canadian Constitution.* Agincourt: Methuen Publications, 1984.

Atkinson, Paul, and Sara Delamont. "Rescuing Narrative from Qualitative Research." *Narrative Inquiry*, 2006: 164–172.

Bains, Ravina. "A Real Game Changer: An Analysis of the Supreme Court of Canada Tsilhqot'in Nation v. British Columbia Decision." *Fraser Research Bulletin—Fraser Insititute.* July 2014. http://www.fraserinstitute.org (accessed July 11, 2014).

Barber, David, and Doug Barber. *Two Ways of Knowing: Merging Science and Traditional Knowledge during the Fourth International Polar Year.* Winnipeg: University of Manitoba, 2009.

Barker, Adam. "From Adversaries to Allies: Forging Respectful Alliances between Indigenous and Settler Peoples." In *Alliances: Re/Envisioning Indigenous-Non-Indigenous Relationships*, by Lynne Davis, 316–333. Toronto: University of Toronto Press, 2010.

Barnhardt, Ray, and Angayuqaq Oscar Kawagley. "Indigenous Knowledge Systems and Alaska Native Ways of Knowing." *Anthropology and Education Quarterly*, 2005: 8–23.

Bar-Tal, Daniel, and Gemma H. Bennink. "The nature of reconciliation as an outcome and as a process." In *From Conflict Resolution to Reconciliation*, by Y. Bar-Siman-Tov, 11–38. Oxford: Oxford University Press, 2004.

Battaglia, Debbora. "Toward an Ethics of the Open Subject: Writing Culture in Good Conscience." In *Anthropological Theory Today*, by Henrietta L. Moore, 114–150. Malden: Blackwell Publishers, 2000.

Bell, Susan E. "Intensive Performances of Mothers: A Sociological Perspective." *Qualitative Research*, 2004: 45–75.

Ben-Ari, Adital, and Roni Strier. "Rethinking Cultural Competence: What Can We Learn from Levinas?" *British Journal of Social Work*, 2010: 2155–2167.

Benoit, Liane E. *On Thin Ice—An Overview of the Governance of Hudson Bay.* Winnipeg: The International Institute for Sustainable Development, 2011.

Berkes, Fikret, Johan Colding, and Carl Folk. "Rediscovery of Traditional Ecological Knowledge as Adaptive Management." *Ecological Applications*, 2000: 1251–1262.

Bhabha, Homi. *The Location of Culture.* New York: Routledge, 1994.

Biehl, Joao, Byron Good, and Arthur Kleinman. *Subjectivity: Ethnographic Investigations.* Berkeley: University of California Press, 2007.

Blackburn, Carole. "Producing Legitimacy: Reconciliation and the Negotiation of Aboriginal Rights in Canada." *Journal of the Royal Anthropological Institute*, 2007: 621–638.

Blackstock, Cindy. "First Nations Child and Family Services: Restoring Peace and Harmony in First Nation Communities." In *Child Welfare: Connecting Research Policy and Practice*, by Kathleen Kufeldt and Bradley D. McKenzie, 331–342. Waterloo: Wilfred Laurier University Press, 2003.

———. "The Canadian Human Rights Tribunal on First Nations Child Welfare: Why If Canada Wins, Equality and Justice Lose." *Children and Youth Services Review*, 2010: 1–8.

Boldt, Menno. *Surviving as Indians: The Challenge of Self-Government.* Toronto: University of Toronto Press, 1993.

Bombay, Amy, Kimberly Matheson, and Hymie Anisman. "The Impact of Stressors on Second Generation Indian Residential School Survivors." *Transcultural Psychiatry*, 2011: 367–391.

———. "The Intergenerational Effects of Indian Residential Schools: Implications for the Concept of Historical Trauma." *Transcultural Psychiatry*, 2013: 320–338.

Bradford, Neil. *Place-based Public Policy: Towards a New Urban and Community Agenda for Canada.* Research, Ottawa: Canadian Policy Research Networks Inc., 2005.

Briggs, Jean, interview by Nadia Ferrara. Personal Communication (April 10, 2000).

Bucholtz, Mary. "Reflexivity and Critique in Discourse Analysis." *Critique of Anthropology,* 2001: 165–183.

Canadian Human Rights Commission. "Canadian Human Rights Commission—Annual Report." *2013 Annual Report.* 2014. http://www.chrc-ccdp.gc.ca/eng/report/issues/aboriginal (accessed August 25, 2014).

Canadian Museum for Human Rights. *Canadian Museum for Human Rights.* August 2014. http://humanrights.ca/about-museum (accessed August 25, 2014).

Carbaugh, Donal. "'Just Listen': 'Listening' and Landscape among the Blackfeet." *Western Journal of Communication,* 1999: 250–270.

Carrithers, Michael. "Anthropology as a Moral Science of Possibilities." *Current Anthropology,* 2005: 433–456.

CBC News. *How Quebec Cree Avoided the Fate of Attawapiskat.* May 14, 2013. http://www.cbc.ca/news/politics/how-quebec-cree-avoided-the-fate-of-attawapiskat-1.1301117 (accessed November 21, 2013).

The Centre for First Nation Governance. *The Governance Toolkit—Best Practices: Osoyoos Indian Band.* 2013. http://www.fngovernance.org/resources_docs/ER_Osoyoos.pdf (accessed July 2, 2014).

Chandler, Michael J., and Chris Lalonde. "Cultural Continuity as a Hedge against Suicide in Canada's First Nations." *Transcultural Psychiatry,* 1998: 191–219.

———. "Cultural Continuity as a Protective Factor against Suicide in First Nations Youth." *Horizons,* 2008: 68–72.

Ciaccia, John. *The Oka Crisis: A Mirror of the Soul.* Dorval: Maren, 2000.

Clifford, James. "Comments on Paul Roth's *Ethnography without Tears.*" *Current Anthropology,* 1989: 555–569.

Collins, Peter. "The Ethnographic Self as Resource?" In *Ethnographic Self as Resource: Writing Memory and Experience into Ethnography,* by Peter Collins and Anselma Gallinat, 228–245. New York: Berghahn Books, 2010.

Corntassel, Jeff, and Cindy Holder. "Who's Sorry Now? Government Apologies, Truth Commissions, and Indigenous Self-Determination in Australia, Canada, Guatemala, and Peru." *Human Rights Review,* 2008: 465–489.

Crean, Susan. "Both Sides Now: Designing White Men and the Other Side of History." In *Response, Responsibility, and Renewal: Canada's Truth and Reconciliation Journey,* by Gregory Younging, Jonthan Dewar, and Mike DeGagne, 62–63. Ottawa: Aboriginal Healing Foundation, 2009.

Cruickshank, Julie. "Negotiating with Narrative: Establishing Cultural Identity at the Yukon International Storytelling Festival." *American Anthropologist,* 1997: 56–69.

Czyzewski, Karina. "The Truth and Reconciliation Commission of Canada: Insights into the Goal of Transformative Education." *The International Indigenous Policy Journal.* August 31, 2011. http://ir.lib.uwo.ca/iipj/vol2/iss3/4 (accessed July 20, 2014).

Dahlgren, Göran, and Margaret Whitehead. *Policies and Strategies to Promote Social Equity in Health.* Stockholm: Institute for Futures Studies, 1991.

D'Andrade, Roy. "Moral Models in Anthropology." *Current Anthropology,* 1995: 399–408.

———. "The Sad Story of Anthropology, 1950–1999." *Journal for Cross-Cultural Research,* 2000: 219–232.

Davidson-Hunt, Iain J., and R. Michael O'Flaherty. "Researchers, Indigenous Peoples, and Place-Based Learning Communities." *Society and Natural Resources,* 2007: 291–305.

Davis, Lynne. *Alliances: Re/Envisioning Indigenous - Non-Indigenous Relationships.* Toronto: University of Toronto Press, 2010.

de Costa, Ravi. "Descent, Culture, and Self-Determination: States and the Definition of Indigenous Peoples." *Aboriginal Policy Studies,* 2014: 55–85.

Desjarlais, Robert, and C. Jason Throop. "Phenomenological Approaches in Anthropology." *Annual Review of Anthropology,* 2011: 87–102.

Devereux, George. *From Anxiety to Method in the Behavioral Sciences.* The Hague: Mouton, 1967.

DeVita, Philip R. *The Naked Anthropologist: Tales from Around the World.* Belmont: Wadsworth, 1991.

Duranti, Alessandro. "Husserl, Intersubjectivity and Anthropology." *Anthropological Theory*, 2010: 16–35.

Durie, Mason H. "Indigenous Knowledge within a Global Knowledge System." *Higher Education Policy*, 2005: 301–312.

Dwyer, Susan. "Reconciliation for Realists." In *Dilemmas of Reconciliation: Cases and Concepts*, by Carol A. L. Prager and Trudy Govier, 91–110. Waterloo: Wilfrid Laurier University Press, 2003.

Epstein, Ronald M. "Mindful Practice." *The Journal of the American Medical Association*, 1999: 833–839.

Ermine, William J. *A Critical Examination of the Ethics in Research Involving Indigenous Peoples.* Master's Thesis, Saskatoon: University of Saskatchewan, 2000.

Ermine, Willie. "The Ethical Space of Engagement." *Indigenous Law Journal*, 2007: 193–203.

Fassin, Didier. *A Companion to Moral Anthropology.* Malden: Wiley-Blackwell, 2012.

———. "Beyond Good and Evil? Questioning the Anthropological Discomfort with Morals." *Anthrpological Theory*, 2008: 333–344.

Feldman, Gregory, and Janine R Wedel. *Mission Statement: Interest Group for the Anthropology of Public Policy.* May 9, 2004. http://aaa-igapp.net (accessed November 13, 2013).

Ferrara, Nadia. *Emotional Expression among Cree Indians.* London: Jessica Kingsley Publishers, 1999.

———. *Healing through Art.* Kingston: McGill-Queen's Press, 2004.

Fine, Gary A., and James G. Deegan. "Three Principles of Serendip: Insight, Chance, and Discovery in Qualitative Research." *Qualitative Studies in Education*, 1996: 434–447.

First Nations and Inuit Health Branch, Health Canada. "Community Development and Capacity Building Curriculum." *Indigenous Community Development.* Ottawa: Government of Canada, 2013.

Fontaine, Phil. "Canadian Race Relations Foundation—Racism and Anti-Racism." *Canadian Race Relations Foundation.* 1998. http://www.crr.ca/en/component/flexicontent/27-racism-and-anti-racism/20977-modern-racism-in-canada (accessed February 14, 2014).

Forget, Marc. "Crime as Interpersonal Conflict: Reconciliation between Victim and Offender." In *Dilemmas of Reconciliation: Cases and Concepts*, by Carol A.L Prager and Trudy Govier, 111–135. Waterloo: Wilfrid Laurier University Press, 2003.

Foucault, Michel. "On the Genealogy of Ethics: An Overview of Work in Progress." In *The Foucault Reader*, by Paul Rabinow, 340–372. New York: Pantheon, 1984.

———. *The History of Sexuality: An Introduction.* New York: Vintage Books, 1990.

Freud, Sigmund. *The Future Prospects of Psychoanalytic Therapy, vol. 11 of The Standard Edition of the Complete Psychological Works of Sigmund Freud.* London: Hogarth Press, 1910.

Geertz, Armin W. "Ethnohermeneutics and Worldview Analysis in the Study of Hopi Indian Religion." *Numen*, 2003: 309–348.

———. "On Reciprocity and Mutual Reflection in the Study of Native American Religion." *Religion*, 1994: 1–22.

Geertz, Clifford. *After the Fact—Two Countries, Four Decades, One Anthropologist.* Cambridge: Harvard University Press, 1995.

———. "Thinking as a Moral Act: Ethical Dimensions of Anthriopological Fieldwork in the New States." *The Antioch Review*, 1968: 139–158.

Gehrke, Pat J. "Being for the Other-to-the-Other: Justice and Communication in Levinasian Ethics." *The Review of Communication*, 2010: 5–19.

General Assembly of the United Nations. "United Nations Declaration on the Rights of Indigenous Peoples." March 2008. http://www.un.org/esa/socdev/unpfii/documents/DRIPS_en.pdf (accessed August 4, 2014).

Gewertz, Deborah B. and Errington, Frederick K. *Twisted Histories, Altered Contexts: Representing the Chambri in a World System.* Cambridge: Cambridge University Press, 1991.

Giabiconi, Julie. "Serendipity...mon amour? On Discomfort as a Prerequisite for Anthropological Knowledge." *Social Anthropology*, 2013: 199–212.

Goodall, Jane, interview by Nadia Ferrara. Personal Communication (October 21, 2010).

———. Personal Communication (April 10, 2011).

Government of Canada. *Aboriginal Affairs and Northern Development—First Nation Child and Family Services Program.* July 3, 2013. http://www.aadnc-aandc.gc.ca/eng/1334326697754/1334326744598 (accessed December 31, 2013).

———. *Justice Laws Website: The Indian Act.* December 9, 2013. http://laws-lois.justice.gc.ca/eng/acts/i-5/ (accessed December 14, 2013).

Govier, Trudy. "What Is Acknowledgement and Why Is It Important?" In *Dilemmas of Reconciliation: Cases and Concepts*, by Carol A.L. Prager and Trudy Govier, 65–89. Waterloo: Wilfrid Laurier University Press, 2003.

Guillemin, Marilys, and Lynn Gillam. "Ethics, Reflexivity, and 'Ethically Important Moments' in Research." *Qualitative Inquiry*, 2004: 261–280.

Gupta, Akhil, and James Ferguson. *Anthropological Locations: Boundaries and Grounds of a Field Science.* Berkeley: University of California Press, 1997.

Halpern, Jodi, and Harvey M. Weinstein. "Rehumanizing the Other: Empathy and Reconciliation." *Human Rights Quarterly*, 2004: 561–583.

Haraway, Donna. "Situated Knowledges: The Science Question in Feminism and the Privilege of Partial Perspective." *Feminist Studies*, 1988: 575–599.

The Harvard Project on American Indian Economic Development. *The Harvard Project on American Indian Economic Development.* 2010. http://www.hpaied.org (accessed July 2, 2014).

Hazan, Haim, and Esther Hertzog. *Serendipity in Anthropological Research: The Nomadic Turn.* Farnham: Ashgate, 2012.

Heidegren, Carl-Göran. "Comments on M. Carrithers' 'Anthropology as a Moral Science of Possibilities.'" *Current Anthropology*, 2005: 449–450.

Henderson, James Youngblood. *Treaty Rights in the Constitution of Canada.* Toronto: Thomson Carswell, 2007.

Holder, Cindy L., and Jeff Corntassel. "Indigenous Peoples and Multicultural Citizenship: Bridging Collective and Individual Rights." *Human Rights Quarterly*, 2002: 126–151.

Holdsworth, Clare, and David Morgan. "Revisiting the Generalized Other: An Exploration." *Sociology*, 2007: 401–417.

Hollan, David. "Emerging Issues in the Cross-cultural Study of Empathy." *Emotion Review*, 2012: 70–78.

Howell, Signe. *The Ethnography of Moralities.* New York: Routledge, 1997.

Idle No More. *IdleNoMore.* 2013. http://www.idlenomore.ca (accessed August 25, 2014).

The Independent. *Canada's 'Femicide Epidemic' Brings Calls for Inquiry.* August 24, 2014. http://www.independent.co.uk/news/world/americas/canadas-femicide-epidemic-brings-calls-for-inquiry-9687855.html (accessed August 24, 2014).

Indspire. *Indspire Institute—Indigenous Education, Canada's Future.* 2014. http://www.indspire.ca (accessed July 28, 2014).

Irlbacher-Fox, Stephanie. *Finding Dahshaa: Self-Government, Social Suffering, and Aboriginal Policy in Canada.* Vancouver: University of British Columbia Press, 2009.

Jacobs-Huey, Lanita. "The Natives Are Gazing and Talking Back: Reviewing the Problematics of Positionality, Voice, and Accountability among 'Native' Anthropologists." *American Anthropologist*, 2002: 791–804.

James, Matt. "A Carnival of Truth? Knowledge, Ignorance and the Canadian Truth and Reconciliation Commission." *International Journal of Transitional Justice*, 2012: 182–204.

———. "Scaling Memory: Reparation Displacement and the Case of BC." *Canadian Journal of Political Science*, 2009: 363–386.

The Jane Goodall Institute. *The Jane Goodall Institute.* 2013. http://www.janegoodall.org (accessed December 6, 2013).

———. *United States Roots and Shoots Program for Indigenous Youth.* Report, Arlington: The Jane Goodall Institute, 2011.

Jane Goodall Institute Canada. 2013. http://www.janegoodall.ca/roots-shoots-in-action-aboriginal.php (accessed October 23, 2013).

Johnston, Patrick. *Native Children and the Child Welfare System.* Research, Ottawa: Canadian Council on Social Development, 1983.

Jones, Alison, and Kuni Jenkins. "Rethinking Collaboration: Working the Indigene-Colonizer Hyphen." In *Handbook of Critical Indigenous Methodologies*, by Norman K. Denzin, Yvonna S. Lincoln, and Linda Tuhiwai Smith, 471–486. Thousand Oaks: Sage, 2008.

Jordan, Karin. "Vicarious Trauma: Proposed Factors That Impact Clinicians." *Journal of Family Psychotherapy*, 2010: 225–337.

Jorgensen, Joseph G. "On Ethics and Anthropology." *Current Anthropology*, 1971: 321–334.

Kelm, Mary-Ellen. *Colonizing Bodies: Aboriginal Health and Healing in British Columbia 1900–1950.* Vancouver: University of British Columbia, 1998.

Kent, Linda L. "Fieldwork That Failed." In *The Naked Anthropologist: Tales from Around the World*, by Philip DeVita, 17-25. Belmont: Wadsworth, 1991.

King, Thomas. *The Inconvenient Indian: A Curious Account of Native People in North America.* Toronto: Anchor Canada, 2012.

Kirmayer, Laurence J. "Embracing Uncertainty as a Path to Competence: Cultural Safety, Empathy, and Alterity in Clinical Training." *Culture, Medicine and Psychiatry*, 2013: 365–372.

Kirmayer, Laurence J. "Rethinking Cultural Competence." *Transcultural Psychiatry*, 2012: 149–164.

Kirmayer, Laurence J., et al. *Guidelines for Training in Cultural Psychiatry.* Position Paper, Ottawa: Canadian Psychiatric Association, 2011.

Kirmayer, Laurence J., Gregory M. Brass, Tara Holton, Ken Paul, Cori Simpson, and Caroline Tait. *Suicide among Aboriginal People in Canada.* Research, Ottawa: The Aboriginal Healing Foundation, 2007.

Kirmayer, Laurence J., Jaswant Guzder, and Cecile Rousseau. "Conclusion: The Future of Cultural Consultation." In *Cultural Consultation: Encountering the Other in Mental Health Care*, by Laurence J. Kirmayer, Jaswant Guzder, and Cecile Rousseau, 333–349. New York: Springer, 2014.

Kirmayer, Laurence J., Cecile Rousseau, Jaswant Guzder, and Eric Jarvis. "Training Clinicians in Cultural Psychiatry: A Canadian Perspective." *Academic Psychiatry*, 2008: 313–319.

Kirmayer, Laurence J., Megha Sehdev, Rob Whitley, Stephane Dandeneau, and Colette Isaac. *Community Resilience: Models, Metaphors and Measures.* Report, Montreal: Jewish General Hospital, 2009.

Kirmayer, Laurence J., Cori Simpson, and Margaret Cargo. "Healing Traditions: Culture, Community and Mental Health Promotion with Canadian Aboriginal Peoples." *Australasian Psychiatry*, 2003: 15–23.

Kitigan Zibi. *A New Accountability Agreement for Kitigan Zibi.* March 2012. http://kzadmin.com/NewsDocuments/468_KZA_AccountabilityDoc.pdf (accessed November 30, 2013).

Kleinman, Arthur. *The Illness Narratives: Suffering, Healing and the Human Condition.* New York: Basic Books, 1988.

———. "Triumph or Pyrrhic Victory? The Inclusion of Culture in DSM-IV." *Harvard Review of Psychiatry*, 1997: 343–344.

Kohn, Tamara. "The Role of Serendipity and Memory in Experiencing Fields." In *Ethnographic Self as Resource: Writing Memory and Experience into Ethnography*, by Peter Collins and Anselma Gallinat, 185–199. New York: Berghahn Books, 2010.

Kohut, Heinz. "The Psychoanalyst in the Community of Scholars." In *The Search for the Self: Selected Writings of Heinz Kohut: 1950–1978. Vol. 2*, by Paul H. Ornstein, 685–724. New York: International Universities Press, 1978.

Krawll, Marcia B. *Understanding the Role of Healing in Aboriginal Communities.* Ottawa: Solicitor General Canada, 1994.

La Barré, Weston. "Preface." In *From Anxiety to Method in the Behavioral Sciences*, by George Devereux. The Hague: Mouton, 1967.

Lac La Ronge, Indian Band. *Lac La Ronge Indian Band Community Plan: Context.* Community Plan, Halifax: Cities and Environment Unit, Dalhousie University, 2012.

Ladner, Kiera L. "Understanding the Impact of Self-Determination on Communities in Crisis." *Journal de la Santé Autochtone*, 2009: 88–101.

Lambek, Michael. *Ordinary Ethics: Anthropology, Language, and Action.* New York: Fordham University Press, 2010.

Laughton, Michael. *Moving from the Personal to the Political: Self-reflexivity and Horizontal Difference and the Role in Intergroup Interaction.* Master's Thesis, Ottawa: Carleton University, 2012.

Lederach, John Paul. "Five Qualities of Practice in Support of Reconciliation Processes." In *Forgiveness and Reconciliation: Religion, Public Policy and Conflict Transformation*, by Raymond G. Helmick and Rodney L. Petersen, 183–193. Philadelphia: Templeton Foundation Press, 2001.

Lemay, Rose, Carol Hopkins, and Bill Couchie. *Indigenous Review of "Making Mental Health Count" Drafted by the Organisation for Economic Co-operation and Development.* Paper for International Network of Indigenous Leaders in Mental Health and Addictions, Ottawa: First Nations Health Managers Association, 2014, 1–10.

Lennon, Kathleen. "Gender and Knowledge." *Journal of Gender Studies*, 1995: 133–143.

Levinas, Emmanuel. *Entre Nous: Thinking of the Other.* New York: Columbia University Press, 1998.

Leviten-Reid, Eric. *Reflections on Vibrant Communities.* Research, Ottawa: Caledon Institute of Social Policy, 2004.

Levy, Jennifer M. "Narrative and Experience: Telling Stories of Illness." *Nexus*, 2005: 8–33.

Llewellyn, Jennifer. "Bridging the Gap between Truth and Reconciliation: Restorative Justice and the Indian Residential School Truth and Reconciliation Commission." In *From Truth to Reconciliation: Transforming the Legacy of Residential Schools*, by M. Brant-Castellano, L. Archibald, and M. DeGagne, 183–201. Ottawa: Aboriginal Healing Foundation, 2008.

Mahmood, Cynthia Keppley. "Anthropological Compulsions in a World in Crisis." *Anthropology Today*, 2002: 1–2.

Martin, Christopher. "Transitional Justice and the Task of Inclusion: A Habermasian Perspective on the Justification of Aboriginal Educational Rights." *Educational Theory*, 2014: 33–53.

Maslow, Abraham, H. *The Psychology of Science: A Renaissance.* South Bend: Gateway Editions, 1966.

Mattingly, Cheryl. "Pocahontas Goes to the Clinic: Popular Culture as Lingua Franca in a Cultural Borderland." *American Anthropologist*, 2006: 494–501.

———. "The Concept of Therapeutic 'Emplotment'." *Social Science and Medicine*, 1994: 811–822.

———. "Two Virtue Ethics and the Anthropology of Morality." *Anthropological Theory*, 2012: 161–184.

Maynes, MaryJo, Jennifer L. Pierce, and Barbara Laslett. *Telling Stories: The Use of Personal Narratives in the Social Sciences and History.* Ithaca: Cornell University Press, 2008.

McCabe, Timothy. *The Law of Treaties: Between the Crown and Aboriginal Peoples.* Markham: LexisNexis Canada, 2010.

McCaslin, Wanda D., and Denise C. Breton. "Justice as Healing: Going Outside the Colonizer's Cage." In *Handook of Critical Indigenous Methodologies*, by Norman K. Denzin, Yvonna S. Lincoln, and Linda Tuhiwai Smith, 511–530. Thousand Oaks: Sage, 2008.

Membertou First Nation. *Membertou Welcoming the World!* June 18, 2014. www.membertou.ca (accessed July 2, 2014).

Menkel-Meadow, Carrie. "Restorative Justice: What Is It and Does It Work?" *Annual Review of Law and Social Science*, 2007: 161–187.

Menzies, Peter. "Intergenerational Trauma from a Mental Health Perspective." *Native Social Work Journal*, 2010: 63–85.

Miller, James R. *Shingwauk's Vision: A History of Native Residential Schools.* Toronto: University of Toronto Press, 1996.

Mishler, Elliot G. *Storylines: Craftartists' Narratives of Identity.* Cambridge: Harvard University Press, 1999.

Montour, Erin, and Stephen Huddart. "Indigenous Partners, not Prisoners." *The Globe and Mail.* December 11, 2013. http://www.theglobeandmail.com/globe-debate/indigenous-partners-not-prisoners/article15854720/ (accessed June 25, 2014).

Morantz, Tobi. *The White Man's Is Gonna Getcha: The Colonial Challenge to the Crees in Quebec.* Montreal: McGill-Queen's University Press, 2002.

Napier, A. David. *Foreign Bodies: Performance, Art, and Symbolic Anthropology.* Berkeley: University of California Press, 1992.

Narayan, Kirin. "How Native Is a 'Native' Anthropologist?" *American Anthropologist,* 1993: 671–686.

Neveu, Lily Pol. "Beyond Recognition and Coexistence: Living Together." In *Alliances: Re/Envisioning Indigenous-Non-Indigenous Relationships,* by Lynne Davis, 234–255. Toronto: University of Toronto Press, 2010.

Niezen, Ronald. *The Rediscovered Self: Indigenous Identity and Cultural Justice.* Montreal: McGill-Queen's University, 2009.

Norton, Rob. *Unintended Consequences: Library of Economics and Liberty.* 2008. http://www.econlib.org/library/Enc/UnintendedConsequences.html (accessed December 1, 2013).

Ochs, Elinor, and Lisa Capps. *Living Narrative: Creating Lives in Everyday Storytelling.* Boston: Harvard University Press, 2001.

———. "Narrating the Self." *Annual Review of Anthropology,* 1996: 19–43.

Ortner, Sherry B. "Theory in Anthropology since the Sixties." *Comparative Studies in Society and History,* 1984: 126–166.

Palmater, Pamela. "Genocide, Indian Policy, and Legislated Elimination of Indians in Canada." *Aboriginal Policy Studies,* 2014: 27–54.

Papillon, Martin. "Aboriginal Quality of Life under a Modern Treaty: Lessons from the Experience of the Cree Nation of Eeyou Istchee and the Inuit of Nunavik." *Institute for Research on Public Policy,* 2008: 1–26.

Parliament of Canada. *Aboriginal Self-Government.* June 17, 1999. http://www.parl.gc.ca (accessed December 27, 2013).

———. "Invisible Women: A Call to Action—A Report on Missing and Murdered Indigenous Women in Canada." *House of Commons Committees.* March 2014. http://www.parl.gc.ca/content/hoc/Committee/412/IWFA/Reports/RP6469851/IWFArp01/IWFArp01-e.pdf (accessed August 20, 2014).

Partridge, Cheryle. "Residential Schools: The Intergenerational Impacts on Aboriginal Peoples." *Native Social Work Journal,* 2010: 33–62.

Peacock, James L., and Dorothy C. Holland. "The Narrated Self: Life Stories in Process." *Ethos,* 1993: 367–383.

Penikett, Tony. *Reconciliation: First Nations Treaty Making in British Columbia.* Vancouver: Douglas and McIntyre Publishing, 2006.

———. *Six Definitions of Aboriginal Self-government and the Unique Haida Model.* Conference Paper, Ottawa: Action Canada Northern Conference, 2012.

Politics, CBC News. *CBC News.* June 26, 2014. http://www.cbc.ca/news/politics/tsilhqot-in-first-nation-granted-b-c-title-claim-in-supreme-court-ruling (accessed June 30, 2014).

Portelli, Alessandro. *The Death of Luigi Trastulli and Other Stories: Form and Meaning in Oral History.* Albany: State University of New York Press, 1991.

Prager, Carol A. L. and Trudy Govier. *Dilemmas of Reconciliation: Cases and Concepts.* Waterloo: Wilfrid Laurier University, 2003.

Reconciliation Canada. *Reconciliation Canada.* 2013. http://www.reconciliationcanada.ca (accessed February 9, 2014).

Regan, Paulette. "A Transformative Framework for Decolonizing Canada: A Non-Indigenous Approach." *IGOV Doctoral Student Symposium,* 2005: 1–10.

———. *Unsettling the Settler Within: Indian Residential Schools, Truth Telling, and Reconciliation.* Vancouver: University of British Columbia Press, 2010.

Rifkin, Jeremy. *The Empathic Civilization.* New York: Tarcher/Penguin, 2009.

Rivoal, Isabelle, and Noel B. Salazar. "Introduction: Contemporary Ethnographic Practice and the Value of Serendipity." *Social Anthropology*, 2013: 1–8.

Rosaldo, Renato. *Culture and Truth: The Remaking of Social Analysis.* Boston: Beacon, 1989.

Ross, Rupert. *Indigenous Healing: Exploring Traditional Paths.* Toronto: Penguin Group, 2014.

Royal Canadian Mounted Police. "Missing and Murdered Aboriginal Women: A National Operational Overview." *Royal Canadian Mounted Police.* 2014. http://www.rcmp-grc.gc.ca/pubs/mmaw-faapd-eng.pdf (accessed August 22, 2014).

Royal Commission on Aboriginal Peoples. *Royal Commission Report on Aboriginal Peoples.* February 8, 2006. http://www.aadnc-aandc.gc.ca/eng/1307458586498/1307458751962 (accessed November 20, 2013).

Salzman, Philip Carl. "On Reflexivity." *American Anthropologist*, 2002: 805–813.

Schaefli, Laura M., and Anne M.C. Godlewska. "Ignorance and Historical Geographies of Aboriginal Exclusion: Evidence from the 2007 Bouchard-Taylor Commission on Reasonable Accommodation." *The Canadian Geographer*, 2014: 110–122.

Scheper-Hughes, Nancy. "Making Anthropology Public." *Anthropology Today*, 2009: 1–3.

Serson, Scott. *Reconciliation: For First Nations This Must Include Fiscal Fairness.* 2012. http://www.speakingmytruth.ca (accessed November 20, 2013).

Shepherd, Robert P., and Karen Persad. *Place-Based Evaluation in a First Nations Context: Something Old, Nothing New, Often Borrowed, and Frequently Blue.* Research, Ottawa: Policy Horizons Canada, Government of Canada, 2011.

Sheppard, Colleen. *Indigenous Peoples in Canada: Understanding Divergent Conceptions of Reconciliation.* Aboriginal Policy Study Papers, no. 4, Montreal: Institute for the Study of International Development, McGill University, 2013.

Shore, Cris, and Susan Wright. "Policy: A New Field of Anthropology." In *Anthropology of Policy: Critical Perspectives on Governance and Power*, by Cris Shore and Susan Wright, 3–39. London: Routledge, 1997.

Shutte, Augustine. *Ubuntu: An Ethic for a New South Africa.* Pietermaritzburg: Cluster Publications, 2001.

Sisters In Spirit. "Voices of Our Sisters In Spirit: A Report to Families and Communities." *Native Women's Association of Canada.* March 31, 2009. http://www.nwac.ca/sites/default/files/download/admin/NWAC_VoicesofOurSistersInSpiritII_March2009FINAL.pdf (accessed August 22, 2014).

Smith, Megan, and Art Sterritt. "Towards a Shared Vision: Lessons Learned from Collaboration between First Nations and Environmental Organizations to Protect the Great Bear Rainforest and Coastal First Nations." In *Alliances: Re/Envisioning Indigenous-Non-Indigenous Relationships*, by Lynne Davis, 131–148. Toronto: University of Toronto Press, 2010.

Sones, Rose. *Cultural Competence in First Nation Mental Health.* Research Report, Ottawa: Department of Health Canada, Government of Canada, 2010.

Spiro, Melford E. "Postmodernist Anthropology, Subjectivity, and Science: A Modernist Critique." *Comparative Studies in Society and History*, 1996: 759–780.

Swanson, Darren, and Suruchi Bhadwal. *Creating Adaptive Policies: A Guide for Policy-Making in an Uncertain World.* New Delhi: Sage, 2009.

Taylor, Donald M., and Roxane de la Sablonniere. "Why Interventions in Dysfunctional Communities Fail: The Need for a Truly Collective Approach." *Canadian Psychology*, 2013: 22–29.

Tervalon, Melanie, and Jann Murray-Garcia. "Cultural Humility versus Cultural Competence: A Critical Distinction in Defining Physician Training Outcomes in Multicultural Education." *Journal of Health Care for the Poor and Underserved*, 1998: 117–125.

Throop, C. Jason. "Articulating Experience." *Anthropological Theory*, 2003: 219–241.

———. "Latitudes of Loss." *American Ethnologist*, 2010: 771–782.

Tomaney, John. *Place-based Approaches to Regional Development: Global Trends and Australian Implications.* Research, Sydney: Australian Business Foundation, 2010.

Treasury Board of Canada Secretariat. *Values and Ethics Code for the Public Sector.* December 15, 2011. http://www.tbs-sct.gc.ca/pol/doc-eng.aspx?section=text&id=25049 (accessed December 11, 2013).

Trevithick, Scott. "Native Residential Schooling in Canada: A Review of Literature." *The Canadian Journal of Native Studies*, 1998: 49–86.

The Truth and Reconciliation Commission of Canada. *They Came for the Children.* Report, Winnipeg: The Truth and Reconciliation Commission of Canada, 2012.

Tsilhqot'in Nation v. British Columbia. SCC 44 (Supreme Court of Canada, June 26, 2014).

T'Sou-ke Nation. 2013. http://www.tsoukenation.com (accessed October 20, 2013).

Turner, Dale. *This Is Not a Peace Pipe: Towards a Critical Indigenous Philosophy.* Toronto: University of Toronto Press, 2006.

Umbreit, Mark S., Betty Vos, Robert B. Coates, and Elizabeth Lightfoot. "Restorative Justice in the Twenty-First Century: A Social Movement Full of Opportunities and Pitfalls." *Marquette Law Review*, 2005: 251–304.

Walker, Ryan, Ted Jojola, and David Natcher. *Reclaiming Indigenous Planning.* Montreal: McGill-Queen's University Press, 2013.

Wedel, Janine. "Ethical Research across Power Divides." *Anthropology News*, 2009: 18.

Wedel, Janine R., and Gregory Feldman. "Why an Anthropology of Public Policy." *Anthropology Today*, 2005: 1–2.

Wedel, Janine R., Cris Shore, Gregory Feldman, and Stacy Lathrop. "Toward an Anthropology of Public Policy." *The Annals of the American Academy*, 2005: 30–51.

Wesley-Esquimaux, Cynthia C., and Magdalena Smolewski. *Historic Trauma and Aboriginal Healing.* Report, Ottawa: The Aboriginal Healing Foundation, 2004.

We Were Children. Directed by Tim Wolochatiuk. Ottowa: The National Film Board of Canada, 2012. Film.

White, Aidan. "Exposing Europe's Decision-makers to Public Scrutiny." *European Voice*, 1996: 18–24.

White, Jerry P., Paul Maxim, and Dan Beavon. *Aboriginal Policy Research: Setting the Agenda for Change, Volume 1.* Toronto: Thompson Educational Publishing Inc., 2004.

———. *Aboriginal Conditions: Research as a Foundation for Public Policy.* Vancouver: University of British Columbia, 2003.

Wikan, Unni. *Resonance: Beyond the Words.* Chicago: University of Chicago Press, 2012.

Wilson, Richard A. "Anthropological Studies of National Reconciliation Processes." *Anthropological Theory*, 2003: 367–387.

Wisdom, Ice. *Angaangaq.* 2011. http://en.icewisdom.com/index.php/category/angaangaq (accessed December 21, 2013).

Wotherspoon, Terry, and John Hansen. "The 'Idle No More' Movement: Paradoxes of First Nations Inclusion in the Canadian Context." *Social Inclusion*, 2013: 21–36.

York, Geoffrey, and Loreen Pindera. *People of the Pines: The Warriors and the Legacy of Oka.* Toronto: McArthur and Company Publishing, 1999.

Yukon Self-Government. *Mapping the Way.* 2012. http://www.mappingtheway.ca (accessed December 27, 2013).

Index

AAA. *See* American Anthropological Association
Abenaki, 17
Aboriginal, 15n1; children, 36; communities, 43, 47n4, 53, 58, 61, 90, 126; community awareness, 109; cultures, 92, 125; governance, 110; governments, 58; groups, 58–59, 90–91; identity, 36; issues, 34; leaders, 94, 120; leadership, 110; organizations, 51; people, 38, 54, 86, 88, 89, 90–92, 93, 98–99, 101n7, 108, 135; policy, 127; research, 23; rights, 36, 90, 101n1, 120; self-government, 58; status, 34; studies, 82; title, 36, 47n5, 91, 101n1; ways of life, 47n5; women, 122, 123; youth, 56
Aboriginal Affairs and Northern Development Canada, 11, 34, 47n6, 58, 86, 94, 108, 110, 118n5, 126
Aboriginal Engagement Strategy, 55
Aboriginal Healing Foundation, 36, 92
Aboriginal Leadership Development Initiative, 110
Abu-Lughod, Lila, 13
academic/activist, 82
accountability, 64, 86, 101n3, 110. *See also* public accountability
acculturation, 29, 124
accumulated loss, 33
action planning, 51

active measures, 34
active participants, 99
activism, 120
activist, 46
adaptation, 53, 64
adaptive policies, 125–126
adjunct professor, 82
advocacy, x, 13, 20, 26n1, 43, 131
advocate, 2, 38, 44, 82, 106–107, 115, 119, 132
affective, x, 41, 44, 128; awareness, 86; domain, 128
affordable housing, 123
agency, 78, 122
aggressive breast cancer, 74
Alberta, 61
Alfred, Taiaiake, 11, 15n2, 15n5, 33, 34, 37, 44, 46, 59, 89, 110, 113, 116, 128, 136
Algonquin, 101; First Nation community, 110
Allen-Meares, Paula, 107
alliances, 46
ally, 38, 100, 105, 137. *See also* settler-ally
alterity of the other, 104
altruism, 131
ambivalence, 76, 128
American Anthropological Association, 66n3, 107
ancestors, 4, 6, 137
ancestral spirit, 19

restoration, 11, 137; resurgence, ix, 8, 60, 113, 120, 128; revitalization, 11, 25, 39, 95, 117, 122, 127; rituals, 108; shame, 11, 44; safety, 128; symbols, 109; traditions, 6, 17, 32; transmission, 53; wounding, 116
culturally-based: healing, 46, 95; initiatives, 123. *See also* community-based healing
Czyzewski, Karina, 88, 120

Dahlgren, Göran, 66n4
D'Andrade, Roy, 22, 105
Dandeneau, Stephane, 125, 127
Davidson-Hunt, Iain J., 61, 63
Davis, Lynne, 113, 122
de Costa, Ravi, 120
The Declaration. *See* United Nations Declaration on the Rights of Indigenous Peoples
decision-making, 99
decolonization, 8, 9–11, 50, 51, 69, 82, 90, 92, 94, 100, 105, 107, 113, 120, 125, 132
decolonize, ix, 9–10, 42, 51, 52, 63, 65, 130
decolonized anthropology, 130
decolonizing imperative, 110
Deegan, James G., 71
dehumanization, 86, 136
Delamont, Sara, 78
de la Sablonniere, Roxane, 11
Department of Aboriginal Affairs and Northern Development Canada. *See* Aboriginal Affairs and Northern Development Canada
Department of Indian Affairs, 25
departmental community plan, 126. *See also* intra-type community plan
dependence: sense of, 34
dependency, 66n13, 110
Desjarlais, Robert, 2, 69, 70
destabilization, 11
DeVita, Philip R., 72
Devereux, George, 69
diabetes prevention, 10, 53
diagnosis, 7, 9, 115
dialectal relationship, 2

dialogic, 105; exchange, 13, 29–30, 32, 43, 44, 114, 130; networks, 44, 62, 63; relationship, 82
dialogical awareness, 31
dialogue, ix, 11, 13, 14–15, 18, 20, 22, 31, 42, 44, 69, 70, 82, 86, 101n3, 111, 116, 117; circle methodology, 94; cross-cultural, 4; intercultural, 46. *See also* truth-telling dialogue
dichotomy, 1–2, 19, 22, 29, 69, 86, 132
dignity, 74, 104, 107, 136, 137
discourse, 22, 29, 44, 46, 65, 77, 88, 113
discursive practice, 42
disembodied empathy, 45
disempowerment, 11
disengagement, 112
doctor-patient power dynamic, 115
dormant-oppressed relations, 112
drawing journal, 50
Duranti, Alessandro, 44
Durie, Mason H., 5
Dwyer, Susan, 95

economic development, 53, 59
ecosystem, 64
eighteenth century, 89
Elder, 4, 6, 9–10, 19, 23, 25, 32–34, 38, 40, 41, 42, 45, 56, 61, 62, 70, 72, 79, 89, 93, 94, 98, 101, 108–110, 112, 116, 118n4, 121, 125, 127, 131; as mediator, 118n4; teachings, xiii, 110, 137. *See also* Haida Elder; Innu Elder; Métis Elder
elliptical in-between, 72
emancipatory change, 127
embodied research, 8
emotional expression, 7
emotional intelligence, 19
empathic: approach, 103, 118n1, 127; awareness, 43; connection, 88; listening, 44, 85; researcher, 129; science, 118n1; scientific research, 128
empathy, 8, 20, 29, 43–44, 57, 72, 86, 101, 117, 118n1, 130, 131, 137. *See also* complex empathy; disembodied empathy
enabler, 11, 13
engagement, 1, 85, 88, 111–112, 135, 137

Enhanced Prevention Focused Approach, 36
environmental stewardship, 64
environmentalist, 56, 66n5
epidemic of femicide, 122
Epstein, Ronald M., 129
Ermine, Willie, 4, 5, 13, 18, 111–113, 127–128
Errington, Frederick, 18, 26
ethical: activity, 116; attitude, 104; code of conduct, 115; commitment, 100, 116; discourse, 103; duty, 103, 113, 127; issues, 82; listening, 88; obligations, 115, 117, 122; practice, 69; principles, 92; responsibility, 8, 82, 103, 104, 105, 107, 108, 113, 114, 117, 120, 129; requirement, 107; self-awareness, 103, 129; space, 13, 18, 103, 105, 111–113, 114, 117, 127, 129; stance, 115, 132; standard, 115; subject, 103, 104; subjectivity, 117. *See also* code of ethics
ethics, 103, 112, 114. *See also* anthropological analysis of ethics
ethnocentric, 3, 86, 90
ethnocentrism, 86
ethnohermeneutics, 70
ethnographer, 8, 22, 69, 82, 108
ethnographic: account, 70, 108; fieldnotes, 22; intervention, 130; interviews, 98; material, 43, 116; research, 107; writing, 81
ethnography, 8, 9, 18, 22, 52, 69, 72, 82, 105, 108, 118n1, 131
ethology, 57, 66n10
ethnohermeneutics, 70
Eurocentric, 1
Eurocentrism, 4, 6
Euro-Canadian, 7, 76, 77, 79
Europe, 114
European, 59, 128; occupancy, 90; settlers. *See* settler
evidence-based policy making, 49
experience-distant, 103, 118n1
experience-near, 103, 118n1; knowledge, 51; process, 100
experiential knowledge, 5, 22, 30, 51, 63, 76, 77, 125
external objective truths, 51

failures, 73
Fassin, Didier, 103, 105, 112
federal: authority, 64; departments, 94–96, 107, 126; funding, 40, 58; government, ix, 11–12, 23, 25, 34, 36, 47n4–47n6, 53, 58–61, 88, 92, 95, 108, 122–123, 126; jurisdiction, 92; leaders, 8; network, 65; process, 110; representatives, 51, 111, 119
feeling-thought, 41
Feldman, Gregory, 52, 64, 66n3
Ferguson, James, 130
Ferrara, Nadia, 4, 7, 8, 9–10, 21, 30, 46n1, 66n1, 79, 115
field, 52, 69, 81, 129–130; experience, 76; research, 57
fieldwork, 8, 18, 22, 71, 72, 80, 81, 108, 129–130
Fine, Gary A., 71
First Nation–to–First Nation Mentoring Program, 10, 55, 116, 118n5
First Nations, 4, 8, 11, 13, 15n1, 15n3, 20, 23, 25, 29, 31, 33, 34–36, 38, 40–41, 44, 47n5, 49, 54, 56, 58, 61, 66n7, 90–91, 94–96, 99, 101n1, 108, 115, 119, 124, 129–130; agricultural database, 62; and Inuit Health Branch of Health Canada, 85, 90, 93, 101n8, 116; artist, 94; children, 36, 46n2, 51; communities, 55, 58, 62, 66n2, 86, 98, 111, 132; cultural values, 51; Elders, 51; families, 51; Health Managers Association framework, 93; leaders, 66n5; partners, 52; social service practitioners, 51
First Nations Child and Family Caring Society, 46n2
First Peoples, 1, 13, 85, 128
first-person virtue ethics. *See* humanist virtue ethics
First World country, 86
Folk, Carl, 53
forced assimilation, 112
Forget, Marc, 101n9, 118n3
Foucauldian ethics, 103
Foucault, Michel, 103, 104
Framework Agreement, 61
French Canadian, 76
Freud, Sigmund, 2

Kirmayer, Laurence, 31, 53, 77, 107, 115, 117, 125, 127, 131
Kitigan Zibi Anishinabeg, 110, 111, 132
Kleinman, Arthur, 7, 70, 76, 77, 105
knowledge broker, 13, 31, 55, 66n6
knowledge-compassion-action-reflection model, 56
knowledge-practice-belief, 53
Kohn, Tamara, 81
Kohut, Heinz, 118n1
Krawll, Marcia, 43
Kumik, 108–110, 112

La Barré, Weston, 69
labor force participation, 58
Labrador, 127
Lac La Ronge, 66n7
Ladner, Kiera L., 58, 60, 66n11
Lambek, Michael, 103, 112, 114, 118n2
land claims, 15n4, 58, 91
land and resource management, 61, 89
land use planning, 51, 55
languages, ix, 1, 5, 6, 10, 36, 89, 120
Lalonde, Chris, 44, 58
Laslett, Barbara, 8, 78
lateral violence, 33, 98, 102n11
Lathrop, Stacy, 52
Laughton, Michael, 20, 86
leadership, 61, 90, 95–96, 110. *See also* indigenous leadership
Leakey, Louis, 57
learned helplessness, ix, 11, 31, 98
Lederach, John Paul, 137
legal reconciliation, 121
legislation, 34
Lemay, Rose, 125, 128. *See also* Rose Sones
Lennon, Kathleen, 20, 86
Levinas, Emmanuel, 103, 104–105, 115, 118n2
Leviten-Reid, Eric, 63
Levy, Jennifer M., 79
life: chances, 130; narratives, 77; review, 73; stories, 78; story methodology, 123; storytelling, 77
Lightfoot, Elizabeth, 101n3
liminal state, 72
listener, 80

listening, 3, 11, 13, 15, 20, 34, 37, 39, 42–46, 49, 76, 79, 85, 88, 101, 104, 107, 108, 119, 130, 131. *See also* empathic listening
Littlechild, Wilton, 121
lived experience, 71, 72, 81
lived narratives, 131
lived realities, 4, 25, 29, 49, 51, 64, 70, 80, 89, 95, 126, 131, 132
Llewwllyn, Jennifer, 136
Lo, Hung Tat, 107, 115
local governance, 62
lodge, 109
longhouse, 12, 94

maggot therapy, 82n3
Mahmood, Cynthia K., 30, 107
Manitoba, 4, 25, 61, 121
Maori, 124
marginalization, 3, 9, 19–20, 23, 123, 124
marine environment, 51
Martin, Christopher, 45
Maslow, Abraham, 118n1
Matheson, Kimberly, 33
Mattingly, Cheryl, x, 78–79, 103, 112
Maxim, Paul, 90, 127
Maynes, MaryJo, 8, 78–79
McCabe, Timothy, 90
McCaslin, Wanda D., 7
McGill University, 76, 120
McKenzie, Kwame, 107, 115
medical expert, 115
medicinal: plants, 62; teas, 62
Members of Parliament on the Special Committee on Violence against Indigenous Women, 122
Membertou First Nation, 60, 66n12
memory, 79, 81–82, 88
Menkel-Meadow, Carrie, 101n3
mental health, 32, 115; clinic, 73, 79–80; professional, 94
mentoring, 112
Menzies, Peter, 90, 107, 115, 116
meta-communication, 30, 44
metanarrative, 113
Methodist church, 25
methodology, 8
Métis, ix, 11, 13, 15n1, 20, 31, 44–45, 49, 54, 90, 96, 101n7, 108, 119, 124,

self-transformation, 41, 72, 82
self-understanding, 115
selflessness, 43
Senchoten, 67n14
senior management, 56
senior managers, 95
sense of belongingness, 19–20, 41, 44, 50, 77, 81, 98, 122, 124, 130, 136, 137
serendipitous experience, 72
serendipity, 72, 82, 130, 132
Serson, Scott, 92
settler, ix, 1, 4, 6, 8, 38, 89, 100, 128, 136; complacency, 86; culture, 128. *See also* indigenous-settler relations
settler-ally, 8, 46, 113, 124
settler symbolic violence, 45
Seventh Generation, 62, 136
shaman, 27n3
shame, 33. *See also* cultural shame
shared history, 113
shared humanity, 8
Shepherd, Robert P., 37, 58
Sheppard, Colleen, 88
Shore, Cris, 52, 64
Shutte, Augustine, 105
Siberia, 27n3
silo, 10, 99, 126; busting, 41
Simpson, Cori, 31
situated knowledges, 53
Sisters in Spirit, 123
sixties' scoop, 31, 46n2
Smith, Megan, 36
Smolewski, Magdalena, 101n6
social capital, 63
social change, 86, 88, 128
social determinants: of health, 53, 124; of well-being, 53, 124
social: development, 53; development policy framework, 51; inclusion, 120, 122; inequity, 112; justice, 120; networking, 126; reconstruction, 86; research, 82; sciences, x, 8, 21–22, 72, 78; scientists, x, 13, 69, 78, 104, 128; suffering, 116. *See also* justice
socio-cultural integrity, 124
socio-economic: conditions, 34; development, 66n12; reconciliation, 121; well-being, 53
socio-political terrain, 114

sociologist, 78
solar intensive community, 62
solar panel, 62
solidarity, 122, 137
Sones, Rose, 44. *See also* Rose Lemay
Sooke. *See* T'Souke First Nation
South Africa, 27n3, 105
South African Truth and Reconciliation Commission, 118n3
South America, 27n3
South Dakota, 56
sovereignty, 66n11, 91, 120
space, 4, 6, 8, 9–10, 49, 94, 108–109, 112–113, 114; symbolic construction of, 2
spirit, x, 8–9, 19, 23, 30, 46, 74, 94, 112, 125, 129, 136, 137; of coexistence, 128; of reconciliation, 131. *See also* ancestral spirit; Sisters in Spirit
spiritual: beliefs, 92; realm, 44; reconciliation, 121; rejuvenation, 109; revitalization, 59
spirituality, 56, 108
Spiro, Melford E., 21, 69
spontaneity, 103
stained glass window, 95, 97
stakeholders, 64
Standing Indigenous Advisory Council, 121
Status Indian, 59
Sterritt, Art, 36
steward of the land, 77
stewardship, 120
storied conversations, 81, 82
storyteller, 56, 108
storytelling, 8, 15, 81, 95, 109
strategic planning, 51
strategic unknowing. *See* willful ignorance
strength-based approach, 10, 95, 124, 125
Strength Weaknesses Threats and Opportunities (SWOT) analysis, 133n4
Strier, Roni, 103, 104–105, 112
sub-Arctic, 4
subjectivity, 69, 70, 72, 78, 104
substance abuse, 86
suicidal ideation, 17
suicide, 11, 31–32, 34, 44, 56, 73, 98; prevention, 10, 53; variability, 58

.

About the Author

Dr. Nadia Ferrara is currently a senior policy manager for the Department of Aboriginal Affairs and Northern Development in the Government of Canada. Prior to this, Dr. Ferrara worked for sixteen years as an art therapist, specializing in working with indigenous peoples. Both as a clinician and a bureaucrat, her mission has been to nurture her own humanity through exploring and examining the humanity of others, founded on the principles of mutual recognition and respect. Dr. Ferrara considers herself an empathic anthropologist contributing to humanistic anthropology. She is strongly committed to processes of decolonization and rehumanization by supporting indigenous people in reclaiming their sense of place and engaging in their cultural revitalization. As a medical anthropologist, she remains on faculty at McGill University as adjunct professor in the Department of Anthropology. She has published two other books on her work with the Crees of Northern Quebec; the first entitled *Emotional Expression among Cree Indians*, and the second *Healing through Art*.